SECRET MAGICAL ELIXIRS OF LIFE
Maria D'Andrea

FREE BONUS DVD... DETAILS INSIDE

Explore The Paranormal Vibrations Of Crystals, Gems And Stones For Good Health, Enhanced Psychic Powers and Phenomenal Inner Strength!

SECRET MAGICAL ELIXIRS OF LIFE

Explore The Paranormal Vibrations Of Crystals, Gems And Stones

by Maria D'Andrea MsD, D.D., DrH

FREE BONUS DVD

TO RECEIVE YOUR FREE BONUS DVD PRODUCED
EXCLUSIVELY AS AN ENHANCEMENT
TO THE INFORMATION PRESENTED IN THIS BOOK
SIMPLY E MAIL OR WRITE THE PUBLISHER

mrufo8@hotmail.com

Tim Beckley, Publisher
Box 753
New Brunswick, NJ 08903

Mention Book Title And
Code 63 With Your Request

www.InnerLightPublications.Com

SECRET MAGICAL ELIXIRS OF LIFE

Explore The Paranormal Vibrations Of Crystals, Gems And Stones

By Maria D'Andrea, MsD, D.D., DRH

Copyright ©1988 & 2012 by Maria D'Andrea
All rights reserved. No part of this book may be reproduced, stored in a retrieval system, or transmitted, in any form or by any means, electronic, mechanical, photocopying, recording or otherwise, without prior written permission of the author.

ISBN 9781606111147
ISBN 1606111140

Art Work By Mark Taylor
"Maria" brand logos by Smith and Smyth Creations LLC
Editorial Direction By Timothy Green Beckley
Additional Editing by Sean Casteel
Manuscript Layout and Design by William Kern
Covers by Tim Swartz

**PUBLISHED BY TIMOTHY GREEN BECKLEY
INNER LIGHT PUBLICATIONS**

DEDICATION AND ACKNOWLEDGEMENTS

To my two loving sons.

Rick Holecek, for his persistence and charismatic ideas.

Rob D'Andrea, for his poignant thoughts and emotional creativity.

To Anthony Tedesco and Lisa Sharvin for their direction and product of my weekly TV series, Spiritual World With Maria.

To Sean Casteel for editorial supervision and my publisher Tim Beckley who has always been a supporter of my metaphysical work.

To William Kern for the newly revised manuscript layout and design, and to Tim Swartz for the splendid new covers for this issue.

As they walk upon their path, may they continue to receive their blessings with Love.

Maria D'Andrea

Table of Contents

PART ONE: Elixirs Of Life: The Power Of The Alchemist

PART TWO: Alchemists Of Old

PART THREE: History Of Alchemists

PART FOUR: Secret Magical Elixirs Of Life
DEDICATION OF THE ORIGINAL MANUSCRIPT
INTRODUCTION—THE TIME HAS COME TO OPEN THE DOOR
FOREWORD TO THE ORIGINAL MANUSCRIPT BY ROBERT D'ANDREA
CHAPTER ONE—THE UNLIMITED CRYSTAL
AMERICAN INDIANS AND THE CRYSTAL
CRYSTALS FOR HEALING
MAGNIFICATION OF YOUR DESIRES
CONTROLLING THE WEATHER WITH CRYSTALS
OBTAINING INNER BALANCE
THE TERMINATED CRYSTAL
CRYSTAL POWER RODS
AS A SHIELD
CHAPTER TWO—CRYSTALS FOR SEEING THE FUTURE
A WORKABLE TECHNIQUE
CHAPTER THREE—SELECTING THE PROPER STONE FOR YOU
HOW THE STONES WORK FOR YOU
STONES AND THEIR INDIVIDUAL USES
CHAPTER FOUR—STONES AS TALISMAN
IMPORTANCE OF A STONE'S SHAPE
BRIDAL RINGS
CHAPTER FIVE—HIDDEN MEANING OF STONES
COLOR OF THE STONES
BIRTHSTONES
ASTROLOGICAL STONES
CHAPTER SIX—GEM ELIXIRS AND HEALTH STONES

THE POWER OF HEALING STONES
CHAPTER SEVEN—MAGICKAL STONES TO HELP CAST A BLESSING
EARTH MAGICK
GEMS AND THEIR RELATED HOURS
EARTH AND WATER SPELL
PROTECTION
WHEN BUSINESS IS BAD
PURIFICATION BATH
PSYCHIC INFORMATION OR FOR INFORMATION ABOUT A PERSON
LOVE SPELL
MONEY DRAWING
LOVE ATTRACTION
FOR GOOD LUCK
TO HELP IN MEDITATION
FOR WEALTH
THE PROSPERITY SPELL
HARMONY AROUND YOU
TO STRENGTHEN SPIRITUALITY
TO GRANT YOUR WISHES
LOVE ATTRACTION
MEDITATION
TO BREAK A HEX
RITUAL TIMES
CHAPTER EIGHT—LAPIS LAZULI: PSYCHIC POWER STONE
CHAPTER NINE—LUCID DREAMS
CHAPTER TEN—PSYCHOMETRY WITH STONES
PSYCHOMETRY
CHAPTER ELEVEN—PREDICTING THE FUTURE
THE PENDULUM
CHAPTER TWELVE—RUNE STONES AS A NEW AGE TOOL
CASTING THE STONES
THE RUNE LAYOUT
MEANING OF THE RUNES
SAMPLE LAYOUT
CHAPTER THIRTEEN—MALE AND FEMALE STONES
CHAPTER FOURTEEN—STONES AS A SPIRITUAL TOOL
A NEW AGE SCIENCE UNFOLDS
CONCLUSION
GLOSSARY
ABOUT THE AUTHOR

The three Magi who traveled afar to behold the newly-born Messiah were definitely astrologers and more than likely alchemists.

Native American tribes always included a shaman or two. Many of them practiced their own form of alchemy which included shape shifting and transforming objects.

Look closely and you will see that these "drums" are not musical instruments but really mirrors which the shamans used for scrying purposes and for communicating with the dead.

Many so called fairy tales, including
"Alice In Wonderland," were actually stories and
lessons pertaining to alchemy.

SECRET MAGICAL ELIXIRS OF LIFE

Great mentalists, occultists and alchemists often had vivid imaginations such as how they conceived the ampitheater of the mind.

ELIXIRS OF LIFE: THE POWER OF THE ALCHEMISTS

Elixirs have always been utilized by people in apothecaries for centuries, mainly for health reasons. Shamans, magi, medicine people, occultists, psychics, wizards, tribal leaders, martial artists, yogis and people from other disciplines have also utilized them to their personal benefit as well as to promote those they are seeking to assist and lead along life's path.

Elixirs are a substance said to have the power of changing ordinary lead, iron, gemstones and other metal into gold or of lengthening life indefinitely. Elixirs were often sought after by ancient alchemists. The energy spent was imbued with Universal Life Force energies through prayers, meditations, formularies and intentions. Elixirs have always been used in conjunction with crystals and gemstones to fortify their powers, which goes to make up the primary basis of this study guide's text.

In a way similar to the make-up of the "sparks of life" sought after by modern chemists, elixirs are universally adaptable. Each culture has its own methods, traditionalists and non-traditionalists alike. Some methods will always be the same because of the universal appeal of the elixirs. Therefore, many of these elixirs have been passed down through generations and this is why they are still in widespread use today.

The word "potion" can also be used interchangeably with the word "elixir." Keep in mind that elixirs are most often used to enhance the power and potency of crystals and all sorts of stones. Since a lot of us already possess crystals and gemstones that we work with psychically, it is our decision to make use of the knowledge we already possess and devote this book to elixirs in the context of the world of crystals and gemstones.

SECRET MAGICAL ELIXIRS OF LIFE

The use of an oil and herb creates the basis of vibrational frequencies. The utilization of such additives greatly magnifies the elixirs. The vibration of oils added to water lends to the practitioner a strong foundation on which to build, oils such as: Frankincense and Myrrh, Jasmine and Rose, Mint and Pine, Rosemary, Patchouli and Magnet Oil. Many of these oils are used to enhance a person's love life, attract positive cash flow and further create better opportunities in their life.

Examples:

Prosperity and Abundance - Cinnamon, Almond, Bayberry, Bergamot, Vervain, Honeysuckle

Purification - Acacia, Sandalwood, Clove, Frankincense, Olive

Energy - Vanilla, Carnation, Rosemary, Peppermint, Mint

Meditation - Hyacinth, Jasmine, Frankincense, Sandalwood

Protection - Wisteria, Patchouli, Cypress, Pine, Oak

Happiness and Joy - Apple Blossom, Tuberose, Lily of the Valley

Love - Gardenia, Geranium, Hyacinth, Rose, Musk

Spirituality - Aloe, African Violet, Frankincense

Success - High John The Conqueror, Clover, Lemon Balm

Desires - Sage, Violet, Sunflower

Herbs can be combined with water, as an example.

Examples:

Love - Adam and Eve, Dill, Elm, Jasmine, Rose, Rose Petals, cinnamon

Spiritual Love - Frankincense, Sandalwood, Sage, Jasmine

Abundance and Prosperity - Orange, Lemon, Almond

Intuitive Ability - Bay, Mugwort, Sage, Frankincense, Sandalwood

Protection - Mint, Pine, Cedar, Basil, Burdock, Tobacco

Peace - Sandalwood, Gardenia, Frankincense, Chamomile

Wisdom - Frankincense, Sage/Sandalwood (combined), Sunflower, Peach, Iris

SECRET MAGICAL ELIXIRS OF LIFE

Rejuvenation - Amber, Vervain, Myrtle, Fern

Success - High John The Conqueror, Cinnamon, Juniper

Dreams - Willow, Jasmine, Sandalwood

The gemstones contained in this book in formulae form can be taken out of the formulae and placed in the elixir recipe.

Examples:

Abundance and Prosperity - Bloodstone, Pyrite, Aventurine, Green Sapphire

Success - Clear Quartz Crystal, Pyrite, Gold

Spirituality - Crazy Lace, Blue Agate, Celestite

Love - Rhodocrosite, Rhodonite, Rose Quartz

Wisdom - the use of elixirs will raise the value of wisdom

Protection - Adventurine, Tigers Eye, Turquoise

Happiness and Joy - Crazy Lace, Turquoise,

Tranquility - Peridot, Carnelian, Diamond

Spiritual Healing - Rose Quartz, Red Jasper, Agate

Energy - Turquoise, Selinite, Clear Quartz Crystal

When utilizing elixirs, you are connected to personal transformation while also assisting in planetary transformation. Formulating elixirs can be for plants, animals, personal power, raising community consciousness or for any other purpose you can imagine. More than one person working on synchronized intent for any purpose gives the elixir more potency. The intent needs to be discussed in detail. The more detail you have, the better the results.

Water is the best conduit and is connected to lunar energies. At times the elixirs are connected to solar vibrations. Some are placed in clear bottles while others are placed in dark ones. The combined frequencies within the elixirs connect to the auric field of the planet, as well as lei lines.

Cellular memory taps into your Universal and Spiritual remembrance. The cellular memory reawakens your Spiritual DNA, thus connecting the elixir to your vibrational field. It is important to utilize these methods and to use them in a simple format. The simpler, the more power behind it. One needs to always have a specific purpose in mind, as this helps you to have a direction. When the purpose is

SECRET MAGICAL ELIXIRS OF LIFE

known, you are clearer and then can apply these tools with proper intentions. This allows you to also be practical when applying these elixirs within the realm of Universal Law.

Elixirs are connected to all the elements (earth, fire, water, air). This also, includes astrological contingencies, such as planets and signs. Consciously working with the elements will heighten, attune and empower you. The realm of spirit creates awareness so that you can be further aligned with the elements. Spiritual magick involves picking a specific goal that you can focus on and then applying specific elixirs to create the results you desire. It is important to be patient and to maintain clarity.

Mediation can help you to find your goal. At times when you may have several goals, you may need insight into which goal should be your priority at this time. Meditation is a tool to help you find your center of being, as in the state of Oneness. Taking three deep breaths prepares you to cross the threshold from your waking state of mind into the deeper zones of the Alpha brainwave levels.

When dealing with talismans and amulets for manifesting and protection, you can consecrate them with the use of elixirs. There are elixirs specifically created and blended for this purpose. When utilizing these elixirs, you have to be very careful that your intention matches the purpose. As an added energy boost, you can also blend in the planetary vibrations and the ruler of the particular hour of the day.

Around the world exist many paganistic tribes who performed a variety of alchemy practices.

Gemstones, herbs and oils are of the earth and these are empowered in and of your faith in the Divine Forces and when coupled with your intentions this in its entirety can produce a profound result.

In essence, you can create whatever you so desire with the implementation of elixirs in combination with other spiritual tools. You can create greater alignment, attunement and self-empowerment when you use these elixirs. Moving forward, the following are the steps to creating the life you desire and truly deserve:

1- Picking your goal

2- Meditating on your goal

3- Creating the elixir that fits your goal

SECRET MAGICAL ELIXIRS OF LIFE

4- Focusing on your intent

5- Achieving your goal

Remember to always stay on a positive Path. Be supportive to others. Trust in Divine Power and when you manifest, remember to also thank Divine Power for working with you.

Some alchemists may have been associated with and sanctioned by the Church.

THE ALCHEMISTS OF OLD
YES, YOU CAN CHANGE YOUR LIFE...
JUST LIKE THE ALCHEMISTS OF OLD!

The word alchemy creates images of medieval times, with black magicians, wizards and alchemists working on attaining the Philosopher's Stone and with it the formula for the Elixir Of Life and the transmutation of base metals into gold. This transmutation was also known to represent the Spiritual Quest. This discipline goes back thousands of years and predates medieval times. It is meant to elevate us all.

Researcher Lee Irwin has stated: "Daoism, as the primary indigenous religion of China, is a highly esoteric tradition. Constructed of many different strands, over several thousand years, Daoism has a complex history of integrating various techniques of meditation, spirit communication, consciousness projection, bodily movements, medicine, and "internal alchemy" with a profound transpersonal philosophy of nature and a metaphysics of human relationships based on an ideal of spiritual transformation leading to immortality."

Alchemy is considered a science containing symbols that combined the mystical view of nature and practical science. It is both a Science and an Art. One technique was to unite opposite elements: water and fire, earth and air, the four primary elements. The fifth element was essence/quintessence, which represented spirit.

Alchemists are the scientists of ancient times as well as modern times. As an example, chemistry originated from alchemy. The word alchemy in ancient Egyptian - al Khem, "a mixture to create a mixture" and gem –"black mud of the Nile," which means "to form from a primary substance." It is a science that deals with transmutation.

Alchemists were known in every race and were people of culture and education. They were considered philosophers and chemists. Alchemy is considered a spiritual journey to elevate man. There is a vision of spiritual perfection. The perfected man would have a high degree of spirituality, perfect health, longevity, without pain and hardships, a balanced life, intellect and all that comes with the idea of perfection. The main goal is to attain to becoming a high spiritual being. However, they were talking less of the physical plane of existence than of reaching spiritual perfection. After all, our physical bodies are only here for a short time in the scheme of things.

It is considered the art of mental ability/control to change the structure of objects to another frequency, another vibrational level. The alchemist strives to utilize mental ability to change universal phenomena. An alchemist works on transmuting within matter, substance, life and energy with thought. This is not as unheard of or unbelievable as it seems. Think in terms of your own belief system. We believe there is power in the Word, which is manifested in verbal or non-verbal thought. If you truly understand this and trust/know that there is power in this form, then you are able to understand the underlying concepts of alchemy.

This art is also looked at as a chemical and spiritual blend to change the alchemists' consciousness to a higher vibrational level by purifying the atoms of the body.

Changes can also be accomplished by understanding how the universe works. Elixirs can be created by understanding how the vibrational frequencies of water are affected by adding a stone or a gemstone to the liquid. When you know which stone to add to the water, for what intent and why it works, then you can incorporate it into your life to heighten your success in endeavors of your choosing.

The intent is to improve your life. The elixir formulae in this book are meant to help you attain a better and better life and to aid in creating more abundance and joy. When you utilize a formula, you know that it works. It has already been proven to work. It is an ancient form of science, of cause and effect. When you repeat the same steps and each time the results are the same, you know that any time in the future when you utilize these steps, the outcome will also be the same.

Your focus is on the outcome always, not on just the steps themselves. Intent is very important, even though the energy of the stones and gemstones are combined with the water to create the desired results. Intent is always a part of any process to create.

SECRET MAGICAL ELIXIRS OF LIFE

Remember that as you utilize these methods, many generations prior to you have also incorporated them successfully. Think of it as being the same as a recipe. If you cook something that comes out fantastic and you repeat the same ingredients every time, you will get the same results. If everyone loves your recipe, you can pass it down and they can recreate it for generations. As long as they stick to the original recipe, the food will always taste the same. If they "improve" on it, the results will be different (and maybe not as good).

Working with elixirs has been passed down through the ages. You simply need to stay with the formulae (recipes) to create the same results.

Alchemy is both spiritual and scientific. Thus it can be inspirational to create an idea of what to look for/ focus on/or have as an intent. Next, one must logically work through various ways to implement these ideas to achieve a goal. The focus is important, so you must stay with your goals until they come to fruition. When you work with alchemy, you create changes and cause movement through understanding nature and working with it.

We have the ability to bridge the etheric realms, tap into our Source and create. I came up with a system I like to call "TAP"©. Think of a triangle pointing up.

1-The bottom left corner is "T" for Thought. Whatever you desire to create, you have to put out in thought (The Word) first.

2- Your thought goes to "A," the Astral plane to start to form.

3- Then, it comes back down to "P" for Physical plane, to form in this physical reality.

There you have "TAP." This is an easy way to remember how we create our reality.

Thought, verbal or non-verbal, is the mental level dealing with the Word.

Elixirs are not limited in their utilization. If you can conceive of an idea, you can create it in your life. With the help of knowledge, you are ahead in your life. Knowledge is power to be used. Not just in crisis, but in everyday life.

They say the grass is always greener on the other side. However, with these elixirs and gemstones, you can be the one on the greener side.

There are numerous alchemists that you may be aware of. As an example, Saint Germaine is also known to be connected to the Violet Flame and considered the Lord of the 7th Ray. This Flame transmutes your problems, your baser self to your higher self. This allows you to move up in your vibrational frequency. One of his divine qualities was alchemy. This Ascended Master transmuted his body at Rakocsi Mansion in the Carpathian Mountains through this knowledge and awareness. Master over himself, he said we all have the ability to do the same. Again, knowledge is power.

The well-known alchemist John Dee was also connected to Queen Elizabeth the First. He worked with varied disciplines connected to this alchemical art. The knowledge in many fields adds to abilities of a higher nature.

His son, Arthur Dee, was also working with alchemy. He became the doctor to Tsar Michael the First of Russia and to King Charles the First of England. These abilities help not only the alchemist but those around them as well.

Another alchemist was Hermes Trismegistus. He was called "The Thrice Great" for his level of knowledge and was credited not only for putting down, in writing, the higher levels of alchemy, astrology and magick, but also for being the founder of the Hermetic Order. The Hermetic Order is a high magickal and spiritual system. This Order had a very intense effect on the Western esoteric arts, incorporating both sympathy (sympathetic magick) and the interconnection between all things.

Magick works whether the alchemist or magi understands the reason behind it or not, but this doesn't mean we should not try to figure it out. To utilize techniques and formulae to work with, simply follow directions and work through vibrational frequencies, electromagnetic fields, energetic fields and ancient knowledge. There is power in these, but if you still want to understand the workings of these fields, it's an added plus. You need to have a respectful attitude toward Mother Nature. We are not controlling nature, we understand it in order to work with it to create positive situations in our lives and to banish/get rid of negative situations.

This is not superstition or conjuring, this is ancient science. We are working with cause and effect. The gemstones, as well as the herbs and oils, have their own energy, which can actually be seen by taking a Kirlian photograph of them. Kirlian photography takes a physical picture of energy fields (auras) emanating from people, animals and objects. Kirlian photos were first invented in Russia for scientific purposes, but are also utilized for psychic readings to give you the information needed to make better decisions in your life by knowing what is occurring at the present and in future times. As you can see, the ancient and modern sciences (alchemy) work hand in hand.

In any case, you are setting up an expectancy to create what you desire as

SECRET MAGICAL ELIXIRS OF LIFE

an outcome, to manifest a better and better life. Expectancy is the battery charger for manifesting. Work with the Laws of Nature, expect it and know that it works. After all, if it has worked for centuries, why would it change results now? Remember to thank Divine Power (or whoever you connect to) for bringing in your outcome.

We maintain the empirical scientific/alchemical approach. Everything is made up of energy in the universe and so we are dealing with the workings of nature. Modern science is not absolute. Alchemy and science both have a spiritual aspect, in that they do not dismiss a Higher Power. If the same formulae works with the same results every time, it does not mean the cause is always understood. Yet, it still works. Some of the causes are still speculative, nevertheless they give you the results.

What really matters is not the situation or circumstance you find yourself in but how you react (re=again, act=take action) to it. You can simply give up. You can run around trying to figure it out or you can stop, assess the situation and put your focus/intent on fixing/changing it to improve. You have all the control. Your mind is a powerful tool. Utilizing elixirs and gemstones, you can create your world to be what you have as a goal. The main issue is deciding on what you want to create. What is your intent/ goal? Think it through before you work on it. It is very important to do ONLY positive work. There is Karmic Law at work: cause and effect, as you sow so shall you receive.

When creating with alchemy and magick, you are also dealing with ancient lore. Much of the lore passed down through the ages still has a valid base in reality. When you sift through some ancient tales, you can see how the core of them makes sense. Such as: looking at the ancient Druids. Merlin/Merlyn was known as a wizard. There was an actual person the stories are based upon. He was a well-known alchemist/magi at the time. Many of the stories about his accomplishments have a firm basis when you look at them from an alchemists/scientists/magickal point of view.

One of the magickal laws is that the more you work on matching yourself with the desired results, the better and quicker it comes to pass. Up to now, your focus was result oriented without the techniques coming into play. Now, the added techniques in this book will help you to achieve the goals you set forth for yourself. Look through this book to see which formulae or elixir works best to suit your intent, making sure you work for the positive at all times.

The power rod, utilizing a crystal, is a very helpful tool. You can also make a wizard's wand for the same purpose, with the same measurements. You need to look for a branch to cut from a holly, willow, peach or oak tree. You can use any tree, but the vibrations for this intent are stronger in these.

*** The rite of making a wizard's wand is very personal and is always made alone. ***

1- Take some time to meditate or at least a few minutes to breathe slowly. Allow yourself to relax so you can be open to your intuition/gut feelings.

2- Next, go where the trees are that you wish to check out for your wand. Walk around and pay attention to your feelings. If you get a good feeling or feel pulled toward a particular tree, go up to it. This is your connection.

3- Mentally ask the tree if it is open to you taking a branch for the purpose of making a wizard's wand. If you get a positive or neutral feeling, then it is a yes. If you get an off feeling, then it is a no. In this case, simply move on to another tree and repeat the process.

4- Next, cut the branch and thank the tree for giving it to you. We always give thanks.

5- At this time, take it home and put it somewhere in direct sunlight or somewhere others won't touch it.

6- The next step is to get a gemstone. Get a clear quartz crystal

7- Place the crystal in a glass of clear water for three days.

8- At the end of the three days, take the crystal out and hold onto the water/elixir.

9- Attach the crystal to one end of the wand with leather, string, cord or any other material made from nature. Artificial/man-made will not work well.

10- As you attach the crystal, focus your intent on this being your wizard's wand and that it will connect to your energies and your focus on any intent you work on.

11- Take the elixir and pour it over the wand to connect it with powerful energies, once again focusing your intent on the purpose of the wand.

12- Visualize or know that white light is coming from above your head, down your arms and into the wand to create a positive wand. You have now connected and energized the wand.

13- You are now ready to utilize it, the same way as in the power rod section.

14- Store it in a safe place where others will not touch it. You can place it in a pouch or wrap it in material of your choosing.

This is a power tool to be used with conscious intent and positive use. Remember Karma.

If you carry stones with wood, as an example, in a medicine bag, mojo pouch or power pouch, combine them correctly. The right wood should be connected to the stones for more power. The woods utilized for the wizard's wand are correct for any alchemical/magickal works.

Such as:

Willow wood with rose gemstones for attracting peace, harmony, universal love into your life

Oak and tiger eye gemstones for protection

Elixirs are known for unlimited uses and, when combined alchemically with stones, have a power source that can be tapped into with your mind/thought/the Word/intent, giving it focused direction. Otherwise the stones and elixirs radiate energy in basically a spherical direction. You want to utilize them more with a laser beam effect.

There is great power in the Word. Learn to use it in a positive way. You are also a tool. Give yourself direction.

There is power in many forms, in many realms. We are in a physical plane, but working from a spiritual, astral reality. There are several dimensions that we can tap into through tools such as gems and elixirs. Remember, that which is unseen can still be effective and utilized. Many seek the Path to only the physical, the seen, and the things they can touch. They think if it cannot be seen, it cannot be real and worked with consciously. However, the way I look at it is that you can't see electricity but you don't put your hand in the socket.

We are in control of ourselves and our intentions create the situations around us. Knowing this, we use tools to help us that were given to us by Mother Nature. It is only a matter of understanding the purpose, the function of things in nature and realizing that we can consciously use them to create a life that we want and deserve. God/Divine Power wants us to be happy and gave us the tools to do so.

Alchemists throughout the centuries have utilized all tools available to better their own, as well as other people's, lives.

There are sacred stones as altars, statues, monuments, stones to carry, to do rituals/rites with, to magnetize other stones (lodestone), to be a battery charger

SECRET MAGICAL ELIXIRS OF LIFE

for other stones and anything placed upon them (selenite) and stones that represent and attract specific intent.

Through some elixirs, it is said that you are working on realigning your spiritual DNA. It is understood in magickal circles that we have two sets. The two sets are the physical DNA and the spiritual DNA. The spiritual one can transform the physical when reaching that enlightened level of being.

When you think of energy, you have to look at it as a never-ending movement. Ever spiraling, spinning and moving. This energy flows through the universe and around us and permeates through us at all times. We are energy in motion. We are not only the universe, but are also a part of it. Everything and everyone is connected. Think of it as a giant spider web. Each person/spirit is on a strand. When one moves, it shakes the strand and thus shakes or moves the others on it. Everything is connected. Think of the ripples in water when you throw a stone into it. It isn't just one ripple, it's several. And so it is with us all. That is why, in alchemy/magick, the Law is that whatever you do, it has an effect on others and situations around you, not just you. Make sure what you do is positive only.

You have access to the etheric realm. Make sure you use some form of psychic self-defense first. Even if it is simply saying –"Divine Power protect me." Then you can utilize tuning-in methods, such as mediation, which is the bridge between the worlds, the two realities of man and spirit.

When you so tune into the spiritual realm, you can hold a gemstone to heighten your contact ability. One such stone is the amethyst; several others are clear quartz crystals, carnelian and selenite.

Another method is to make an elixir by placing one of those gemstones into clear water and leaving it in direct sunlight for three days. Next, utilize the water by placing a few drops or just wetting your third eye (center of forehead), your heart and use the rest for rinsing your hands.

Alchemy utilizes advancing the spirit through understanding and working with primal force, which is in all matter. Hindus call it Kundalini. It is also known by other names, such as: Secret Fire, Serpent Fire and Spiraling Energy. This energy is said to spiral upward through the spine. I personally felt it coming down through my spine, but there was still a spiral feeling among the other senses.

These alchemists were thought to be dreamers by some, and were viewed even more negatively by others. The truth is, present day scientists will acknowledge that the alchemists were the philosophers, physicists and chemists who brought forth the sciences we know today. They were the seekers of truth and

SECRET MAGICAL ELIXIRS OF LIFE

were self-driven to prove, improve and light the way for others.

At the same time, they were always underground on many levels. This power can be utilized in both positive and negative forms. It depends on the alchemist which way the decision will be. Such power is always sought after. It is meant to purify and elevate and therefore not to be given into the wrong hands, under any circumstances, just like a parent who doesn't let a child play with fire. It was to be protected and passed down. Many of the writings on alchemy are in code. If you are in the know, you will understand it, otherwise it is meant to be obscure.

Fire energy is very different from water energy, as an example. Water flows with emotional energy. It works with intuition – a passive energy of receiving information, of being a container of energy. Fire is active; it burns and transmutes the baser soul into the higher spirit. Fire represents the Eternal Flame, energy, warmth, light and destruction (much like the Phoenix bird which burned into ashes and was reborn). You have to destroy the negative and reform it into something positive.

Fire also transmutes the negative feelings of fear into the positive ones of love. Love is a powerful universal force. The alchemical fire within is a force to be reckoned with and utilized by focusing your intent.

The seeds of life are in all of nature, ready to grow and expand. We simply need the techniques to be able to work with them to create whatever we desire. The holographic universal energies encapsulate all living and non-living things. We simply know how to work with them. Elixirs and stones are some of the many disciplines we utilize.

We should all be thankful that the alchemists of ancient times paved the way for the ones in modern times. Science has proven much of the information passed down through the ages as being valid. We, in the spiritual fields, are always open to confirmation, but that does not mean we need the confirmation. We already knew and have worked with ancient knowledge all along.

Techniques and knowledge are the keys to working with the ability to manifest a better and better life. The more you work with elixirs, the more you will find life getting easier and more under your control. The gemstones all have their own vibrations and specific frequencies. They are tuned into universal cosmic energies.

Love is the strongest universal force and working from it also heightens your abilities. This force adds to your power. However, all the formulae in this book work on vibrational frequencies and have ancient power of their own. They work

SECRET MAGICAL ELIXIRS OF LIFE

whether you believe in them or not. The power source is in nature itself. All people, plants, animals, material things, the universe, ALL things are made up of energy. We are all connected. Think of a white strand of energy connecting us all. Knowing how to work with these energies, pulling/pushing/swirling, can transmute your life to one that is extraordinary.

The simple act of utilizing water combined with gemstones can create the effects you desire, easily and effectively. Alchemy, gemstones and elixirs will be with us until the end of time. Utilize the knowledge to your advantage. Bring out the alchemist in you.

Create your world now!

HISTORY OF ALCHEMISTS

Some consider them to be charlatans.

Others believe them to be among the most magical and powerful men on the planet.

Their claims of having obtained eternal youth and the ability to turn low-grade metals into gold and valuable gems have caused a great deal of hullabaloo over the centuries. But indeed, despite its controversial nature, is there anything to the claims of alchemists, that they can create jewels and gold by employing what is known as an alchemist's oven? Is it indeed possible to shove in some base substance, poke it around in the extreme heat and open a trap door out of which fall items greatly increased in value which can be adorned by all who can accomplish such feats almost as easily as saying one, two, three.

Now alchemy in some respects is like the manifestations in spiritualism. There are some who claim to be physical mediums. This means they can conjure up the dead and have their sprits walk around the room. They accompany this remarkable feat with levitating tables, floating trumpets and actual conversations with the deceased. Other spiritualists are more reserved in their convictions. And, while they may believe in the possibility of physical manifestations, they are more inclined to promote the spiritual aspects of the phenomenon. They talk about the phenomenon in more or less abstract form, how a belief in life after death can lead to a spiritual awakening, to a lofty plateau of understanding and knowledge of the way in which the cosmos works.

Alchemists were no different.

Some proclaimed they had become masters of the transmutation of ordinary metals and stones and could turn such a stash into a cache of gold and lavish jewelry. They also tried to convince the world that their alchemic formularies could

SECRET MAGICAL ELIXIRS OF LIFE

be used as an elixir of life – that it was possible to become immortal if one only possessed and utilized the right cosmic principles Others played down the sensational, physical, aspects of alchemy, being more at ease with talking about how alchemy was simply a tool that would lead to an inner understanding of the ages, bringing about a higher plateau in one's otherwise mundane existence.

BECKLEY ON HIS FAVORITE ALCHEMISTS

Lucky me! It turns out that my publisher, Tim Beckley, knows a little something about the history of alchemy and the alchemists, sometimes controversial figures in their own right, who popularized the process of transmutation, the Philosopher's Stone, and the elixirs of life that we are justifiably engrossed in. So I said to myself, hey, let me curl up and read a good book, sip a glass of fine wine from my favorite Hungarian vineyard, and let him work his posterior off like I do. I asked him to provide us all with a list of his favorite top alchemists of all time and he was happy to comply.

Count Saint Germaine is perhaps the most famous alchemist of all time.

COUNT SAINT GERMAINE

Probably the best known and most venerated alchemist is the International Man Of Mystery, the 18th century alchemist by the name of Count Saint Germaine who many believe may still be alive today at well over 400 years old! The Count was respected in "high quarters" throughout all of Europe. He hobnobbed with the likes of Catherine the Great and Marie Antoinette, presumably before she was hobnobbed by a guillotine. He was courted by royalty not only for his miraculous feats of alchemy but because he was a fashion magnet and dressed high brow. It is said he had jewels popping out of every buttonhole and pocket, although he had no visible means of income, not having worked a day in his known lifetime.

Other "facts" include his being at the signing of the U.S. Constitution and at the Treaty of Versailles. I have even heard he has a seat at the UN, but that I find to be preposterous.

SECRET MAGICAL ELIXIRS OF LIFE

A control of the elements all around him made Albertus Magnus a well seasoned alchemist.

ALBERTUS MAGNUS

It's a wonder Albertus Magnus wasn't burned at the stake as a witch.

I guess he got away with his alchemistic research by being a devoted man of the cloth, that is, a Catholic Bishop and ultimately a Saint. He was among the first to try to balance the absolutes of the Church and the letters of science. He left behind a virtual encyclopedia of 38 volumes on botany, geography, astronomy, astrology, mineralogy and chemistry. And, man, if you ask me that's saying an awful lot in anybody's book.

As far as the alchemy part of his career goes, Magus is said to have discovered the Philosopher's Stone that allows devotees to become immortal. I suppose he didn't want the world to be overpopulated because he only passed this knowledge down to his most trusted students. Not reading Latin and not being privy to the inner sanctums of the Vatican's archives, I've never had the opportunity to browse through his *De mineralibus*, a reputed commentary on the esoteric usage of stones in alchemy. I asked Maria if she had ever perused this "article of faith" and she just looked at me rather strangely. I would assume that writing on the subject of alchemy and elixirs, she could recite Albertus's text throughout. Guess she doesn't read Latin either!

Albertus was also said to be a rather astute student of astrology. If he could see into the future, he might realize that Maria and I are referencing him many hundreds of years into the future and he can therefore bless our rather troubled and certainy exhausted souls.

SECRET MAGICAL ELIXIRS OF LIFE

Frances Bacon wrote on many arcane topics. Many believe him to be the quill behind Shakespeare.

FRANCIS BACON

By this time I assume that everyone knows that Francis Bacon was also the literary soul of William Shakespeare. If you have read Sean Casteel's tract on the subject, "To Be Or Not To Be" (available on Kindle), you will realize that the Bard was not capable of such literary virtuosities as he was poorly educated and certainly no master of Middle English. Bacon, on the other hand, was a real "know it all" – and I do mean that literally and in a positive sense. The reason for such a disquise was simple – Bacon had established a reputation with those in "high places" and he didn't want to ruin that connectivity. He wanted to sort of stay in the shadows and work behind the scenes to foster his noble ideal for a New Age of equality and globalism.

On the subject of alchemy, in the year 1627, Francis jolted the European uppercrust with his self proclaimed *Sylva Sylvarum* on the making of gold. It is not an easy work to decipher and it almost appears to be written in code. Or maybe it's just too over my head. But then Alchemists often tried to confuse the uninitiated so as to keep their secrets close to their vest.

We do know that Bacon has often been widely "accused" of being a Freemason as well as the "Imperator" (leader) of the Rosicrucian Order in all of Europe. Some of his musings on "divine and human understanding" were best rectified and expressed in his *New Atlantis,* a widely circulated, novelistic proclamation about a "lost land" with futuristic ideals for its day and age.

SECRET MAGICAL ELIXIRS OF LIFE

DOCTOR JOHN DEE

I would consider Englishman John Dee to be one of the most accomplished alchemists and magicians of all time. Maybe it has something to do with the fact that we share a common birthday (July 13). In his life he mastered numerous sciences, including mathematics, astronomy, astrology, as well as various aspects of the occult. In his early years he spent countless hours in dreary research mainly in the disciplines of Christian studies and math, for which he did receive a degree of acknowledgement from Trinity College, where he was made a founding fellow.

Dee maintained a rather complex understanding of the cosmos which was not acceptable to many factions of the rather dogmatic Church. In 1555, Dee was arrested and charged with "calculating," which means in layman's terms that he was caught casting the horoscopes of Queen Mary and Princess Elizabeth; the charges were expanded to treason against Mary. Dee appeared in the Star Chamber and exonerated himself, but was turned over to the Catholic Bishop Bonner for religious examination.

Almost impossibly, it seems things went from bad to worse.

Dee had developed a cryptic system of communicating with angels which certainly would have been a No! No! at almost all social strata levels. Dee maintained that the angels laboriously dictated several books to him this way, some in a special angelic or Enochian language. If this doesn't give him credentials for being a bona fide alchemist, I don't know what does. In addition, Dee and his "associate" Edward Kelly, a noted clairvoyant of mixed repute, apparently came into possession of a large quantity of the Elixir identified as Red and White Tinctures in the ruins of Glastonbury Abbey. History records that during that time, Kelly took a small amount of mercury and produced nearly an ounce of the best gold.

Many, including the infamous Aleister Crowley, have attempted to duplicate Dr. Dee's "language of the angels" to capitalize on the rewards it offered – mainly a pocket full of gold, I would suppose!

SECRET MAGICAL ELIXIRS OF LIFE

ALEXANDER SETON THE SCOT

Believe it or not, Alexander Seton was a Scottish researcher who travelled around the European continent for several years after 1602, giving public demonstrations in many major cities. At these open events, he performed transmutations of base metals to gold, usually in the presence of many observers.

There is ample evidence to show that alchemy was – and is – not a figment of one's imagination, not a fantasy, not a fraud (at least in some instances). It has been spoken about with great reverence even within orthodox religion, at least among the educated adepts who are prone to keep the entire matter from the public for fear the wealth would be spread too far. Not much is known about Pierce, the Black Monk, except that he wasn't black but a member of a Catholic order and that he penned the following in 1040 A.D. on the Elixir of Life:

"Take earth of Earth, Earth's Mother, Water of Earth, Fire of Earth and Water of the Wood. These are to lie together and then be parted. Alchemical gold is made of three pure souls, purged as crystal. Body, soul, and spirit grown into a Stone, wherein there is no corruption: this is to be cast on Mercury and it shall become most worthy gold."

We don't know if Pierce was persecuted because of his bold statements on transmutation, but certainly others were, such as Alexander Seton, familiarly known as The Scot. In fact, in *The History Of Alchemy*, it has been said that he "suffered indescribable torments for his knowledge of the art of transmutation. After practicing in his own country, he went abroad, where he demonstrated his transmutations before men of good repute and integrity in Holland, Hamburg, Italy, Basle, Strasbourg, Cologne, and Munich. He was finally summoned to appear before the young Elector of Saxony, to whose court he went somewhat reluctantly. The Elector, on receiving proof of the authenticity of his projections, treated him with distinction, convinced that Seton held the secret of boundless wealth. But Seton refused to initiate the Elector into his secret and was imprisoned in Dresden. As his imprisonment could not shake his resolve, he was put to torture. He was pierced, racked, beaten, scarred with fire and molten lead, but still he held his peace. At length he was left in solitary confinement, until his escape was finally engineered by the Polish adept Sendivogius. Even to this dear friend, he refused to reveal the secret until shortly before his death. Two years after his escape from prison, he presented Sendivogius with his transmuting powder"

No doubt my friend Timothy could wax more eloquenlyt on a subject he enjoys so much. I believe I've seen his light on rather late at times in his Manhattan castle. No doubt he is experimenting with transmutations and must be successful or how would he be able to publish so many great works in the metaphysical field?

But let us leave Mr. Beckley to sort his gold and venture forth now with our own elixirs and ultimately finding our own Philosopher's Stone.

It is recommended at this point that you play the DVD that either accompanies this book or that you may obtain without cost by emailing or writing the publisher.

mrufo8@hotmail.com
Tim Beckley
Box 753
New Brunswick, NJ 08903

Aleister Crowley was greatly influenced by alchemy and in particular the supposed ability of Dr. Dee to communicate with a variety of entities.

SECRET MAGICAL ELIXIRS OF LIFE

NOTES

SECRET MAGICAL ELIXIRS OF LIFE

PART FOUR: SECRET MAGICAL ELIXIRS OF LIFE

Explore The Paranormal Vibrations Of Crystals, Gems And Stones

by Maria D'Andrea MsD, D.D., DrH

INTRODUCTION
THE TIME HAS COME TO OPEN THE DOOR

Isten hozott – God brought you to me, as we say in my native Hungarian.

In man's unending quest for knowledge of self, he is rediscovering the ancient sciences and the lost arts which actually were never really lost. Much of the ancient information was either not widely known by the general public or was secretly practiced by a select few.

In addition, because of changing political climates, the information at times had to go underground, and it is just now, with the widespread interest in anything classified as "New Age," that people are sincerely beginning to seek out that which has remained dormant for so long.

The hidden value of crystals, as well as other natural stones and gems, was recognized by what we have come to think of as "primitive man," and they have once again only begun to surface in the light of recent developments in alternative thinking.

As we shall discover, each stone has its own characteristic vibration which when tapped into can produce much needed spiritual, emotional, mental and physical change in the wearer. Stones were and can be used for many purposes besides just being attractive in their own right. In addition t being really fun to own, they can bring their owner success, good fortune, love and a wealth of other benefits.

Indeed, crystals and stones can be used to attract the better things to you. For example, the vibrational properties of crystals and gemstones are known to aid in meditation, while other stones are used in healing, for protection, to prevent psychic attack, and so forth.

Stones, as we shall find out, have varied effects on different people. It depends in part, upon the compatibility of the individual's vibration with the vibration of the stone.

Gems and stones of all kinds act as magnets that draw the characteristic vibration of the stones to its wearer. Because stones take time to build up an energy charge, their total results and effects may often take time to materialize.

The author would like the readers to experiment with the information contained within this book so that they, too, can see and feel the effects of the vibrations of the stones on themselves, their family and their friends. I sincerely hope the knowledge within these pages will help to enhance your awareness of the world and universe that exist around each and every one of us.

May God Bless You Abundantly.

Love & Light
Maria D'Andrea

FOREWORD

By Robert D'Andrea

Maria D'Andrea is a world renowned psychic who specializes in reading runes, tarot cards and using Crystals, Gems & Stones. She knows all the different kinds of crystals and how to use them, as well as how to figure out which one is best for you. There is so much to learn in this field and Maria, in my opinion, is very qualified to pass along this knowledge to you. Plus, she is a good teacher. I know you will enjoy and learn a lot from this book. I know I did and everyone I know who has read this book learned a lot, too.

CHAPTER ONE

THE UNLIMITED CRYSTAL

The clear white quartz crystal is the most versatile stone known. It is virtually unlimited in its uses.

When the quartz crystal is carried it deflects negativity, heightens spirituality, heals, increases psychic awareness, and may be used to predict the future. It is also used to communicate with other people and with spirits through telepathy. And while the psychic benefits of crystals are being highly praised these days, many of us are not aware of how much our culture has become dependent on them in a scientific and technical sense.

Among the varied uses are: microwaves, watches, computers, as monitors in space travel and air flight, as well as microphones and other communications devices.

Going back many centuries in time, there are those who state flatly that crystals were used on the lost continents of Atlantis and Mu, and that when applied in a beneficial way brought great wisdom to these ancient people, but when used unwisely may even have caused the downfall of these great civilizations.

AMERICAN INDIANS AND THE CRYSTAL

As an honorary member of the Tuscarora Indian tribe, I have had numerous talks with Chief Wise Owl on the subject of quartz crystals and how they were often used by the Native Americans as a source of power.

The Native Americans, I have constantly been reminded, have always found it personally beneficial to carry crystals with them in their medicine bags. They believe that when carried for a long period of time it builds up a protective force shield for its keeper, and that it will send back any negative thoughts or wishes to the person who set them out.

CRYSTALS FOR HEALING

Most frequently, when we think of crystals today, we think of them in terms of tools for healing. To keep yourself in tune with the universe it is only necessary to wear a crystal around your neck. Another way to stay in balance is to keep a clear crystal under your pillow for seven nights. Before placing it there it is a good idea to energize the crystal. You may do so by holding it in your hand and concentrating all your energy into the crystal. If you wish to heal a specific part of the body, aim the crystal at the part of the anatomy that is in poor health. Move it in a circular pattern for 10 to 15 minutes over this area, going in a clockwise direction. If you are doing a healing on someone else, turn the crystal so that its point is directed toward that other person. Make sure to hold the crystal under running water when you have completed the healing process so that it can be stored for later use on someone else.

When working with crystals for healing purposes it is important to visualize the pain leaving the body. With the point of the crystal held downward, run the crystal over the troubled area six or seven times, and remember it isn't necessary to actually touch the body as a clean sweep over the ailing limb will do just as well.

To program your crystal to heal, write on a piece of paper what it is you specifically wish the crystal to accomplish. Wrap the crystal in the paper and leave it alone for two or three days. Do not use this crystal for any other purpose than for the healing you have planned. You can also tape a healing crystal over the area that needs the healing, or suspend the crystal over the area.

With a little bit of practice you should be able to help yourself as well as those you love who are in pain, but always remember to see a doctor as this is your best source for medical attention.

MAGNIFICATION OF YOUR DESIRES

Regardless of the nature of your desires, you can magnify what you want to have attracted to you by working with a crystal. Whether it is a new relationship or money, hold the stone between your fingers and look into its depths. Concentrate on what you seriously would like more of and then breathe upon your crystal. For you see, there is power in your breathe and now all you have to do is wear the crystal, or carry it with you. It is as though you just sent out a very powerful request to the universe and you need only to wait and your requests will be met.

I had a client who simply adored the house his best friend lived in and wanted very much to have one like it. Six months later, his friend was made a better job offer and decided to move. He would be making a lot more money and he wanted to move closer to where he would now be working. He remembered how much his friend always admired his home and so he offered it to his buddy at a lower price than he would have asked of anyone else. Soon my client received the exact house he wanted, and it not only benefited him, but also his friend who got the property on and off the market and arranged for the closing in no time at all.

This is a good point to note that when working with crystals you should use them only in a positive, constructive way. The laws of the Universe are very real and they must be dealt with accordingly. You need to always remember that nature is not forgiving. It does not have any middle ground, so if you abuse it there will be a definite paying back to do in the near future.

CONTROLLING THE WEATHER WITH CRYSTALS

There is every indication that the weather can actually be controlled through the use of crystals. One of the methods crystal advocates are using is to hold a quartz crystal in your hand and aim the point towards the sky. It is best to pick a day when the sky is clear and you can visualize small fluffy clouds forming. You have to want it and feel it happening. After a short time you will see the beginning effects. Keep concentrating until you have formed an entire cloud. It may take a few tries, but do not give up. You may want to form rain clouds and then rain, especially if there has been a long dry spell and you need it for growing. It is important that you do NOT fool around with Mother Nature because you do not want to disturb the tender balance of nature. Nothing in nature is a coincidence, everything has a reason even though there are those among us that have not learned this fact yet.

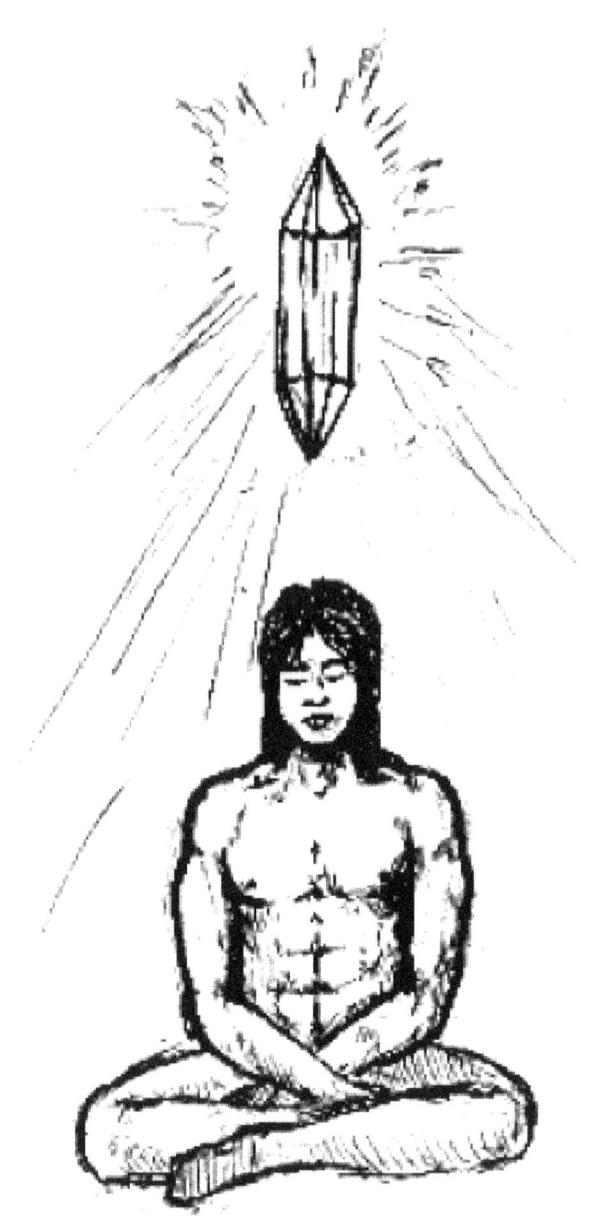

OBTAINING INNER BALANCE

The quartz crystal can also be used for obtaining inner balance. When meditating, researchers have noted that a person's psychic centers - or chakras as they are known in the East - open up a lot faster when a clear quartz crystal is placed side-by-side with a dark quartz crystal (such as a smokey quartz).

Such a process puts you in tune with your inner self and thus the Universal mind. Over a period of time, you can raise what the Yogis call the Kundalini or Serpent Power within yourself. There are seven major chakras or energy vortices that appear as tiny spinning wheels of energy. There vortices hold the etheric body into the physical body and when your chakras are unblocked it allows you to express your full potential as a child of Divine Power. You have always been a perfect expression of the Divine, but only now are you able to project it outwardly.

It is possible to activate the crystal to balance your chakras. Hold a quartz crystal in your left hand palm up with the point facing down. Tighten your hand around the crystal just a little and you should feel the energy flow through you. This technique will help balance your system and lead to improved personal health and spiritual growth.

THE TERMINATED CRYSTAL

No two crystals are identical, just as no two snowflakes ever are. Actually, there are many varieties or types of crystals, one of the most popular being the terminated crystal. These crystals grow beneath the ground suspended in red clay and are composed of six angles or facets and six sides, ending in one point (terminated), or a point on both ends (double terminated). They are considered much as a phone wire that connects us to a higher consciousness, with us on one end and communicating with the Higher Realms who are on the other.

The strongest energy focus of any crystal is at the point. If held to your Third Eye - located in the middle of the forehead with the point placed up, the crystal can be used for past life recall and reception as well as for telepathy. It is said that this method was used in Atlantis. The priestess would go up into the mountains, raise her arms toward the sky and wait for the crystal to be activated. Anyone viewing this at the time would assume that the priestess was praying or communicating with God, when in all actuality she was simply communicating to the world she originated on.

SECRET MAGICAL ELIXIRS OF LIFE
CRYSTAL POWER RODS

One of the methods of utilizing crystals is still being applied today by those who have tried to tap into this ancient energy. Known as the Crystal Power Rod it is quite commonly believed that such great prophets as Moses, Merlin and possibly even the French seer Nostradamus used it in accomplishing their great feats. By reading the Bible we can learn much about the "power rod" Moses performed his miracles with. Nostradamus and Merlin, on the other hand, used a crystal device which stood on a copper tripod to divine the future. There is no reason why modern day man cannot perform such feats and perhaps do them even one better!

The Crystal Power Rod is in reality a chamber that collects sub-atomic particles that when discharged can control the weather, send thoughts or power through space, and can even be used as a lethal weapon. Because of this, only those who are of true spiritual mind should undertake the task of making such a potent device.

To build a Rod of this type you need one foot of copper tube which is of an inch in diameter. On one end of the tube you glue on a copper cap. On the other end you need to place a terminated quartz crystal that is clear and flawless. You insert the crystal three quarters of the way into the tube with the point sticking out. Then you glue it into place. Next, wrap copper wire around the tube starting a little above the crystal all the way to the cap. When this has been done, cover the middle of the Crystal Power Rod with a leather piece as this will keep it insulated for when you hold it.

As soon as you take hold of the rod you are activating it. Visualize what your need is, add your strongest emotions and picture the White Light coming form above your head, down to your throat, and through your arms, then hands into the Rod. This is how you go about storing the cosmic energy. When you are ready to use it, aim the Rod in the direction you want and it will work much like a laser beam. The Rod is actually what focuses the crystal. If used correctly it is more powerful then a laser beam.

Several years ago one of my clients made a Power Rod and decided to use it for destructive purposes, even though he had been warned of the possible consequences. He wanted very badly to get rid of a business competitor and so he visualized the other persons business being destroyed. However, as I stated earlier, you get back what you send, and in the course of the next couple of weeks the competitor started to build his business back up while the owner of the Power Rod started to go broke. His reputation was being questioned and within a short while he had to file bankruptcy.

If he had used this device in a positive way and hadn't tried to harm someone else's business, he would have profited in the end. So, as you can see, as with any warrior, you can use your weapons that you have at your command in either a defensive-positive or offensive-negative way. You should make the choice extremely carefully.

AS A SHIELD

The Crystal Power Rod can also be used as a shield or a strong protection device. To make such a shield, take four terminated quartz crystals and place them around your house, one at each end of the compass (i.e., North, South, East and West). You can also use crystal clusters for the same purpose. Either way, place the stones three quarters of the way into the ground, and then anytime you need to use the shield concentrate on a dome of white light covering your home. Touch each stone and affirm that nothing harmful can penetrate your shield.

NOTES

CHAPTER TWO
CRYSTALS FOR SEEING THE FUTURE

The history of scrying is well known. Crystal balls have had their place in kingdoms far and wide throughout history, and gifted individuals have been trying to determine the future for thousands of years with crystal ball gazing being the most popular method.

Some sensitives prefer a ball that is nearly as clear as possible, while other psychics say a ball that is at least slightly cloudy works best for them. In Tibet the priests would spend a good portion of their lives polishing specially selected crystal balls. Today such a ball might cost hundreds of dollars depending upon size and clarity.

SECRET MAGICAL ELIXIRS OF LIFE
A WORKABLE TECHNIQUE

Today, many psychics have turned in their crystal balls and are reading crystals of all shapes and sizes. You will want to do whatever works best for you and what makes you feel the most at ease. In any case, to make this technique work you will need a crystal that is as nearly flawless as you can obtain. This is very important; otherwise you may get confused or unfocused information.

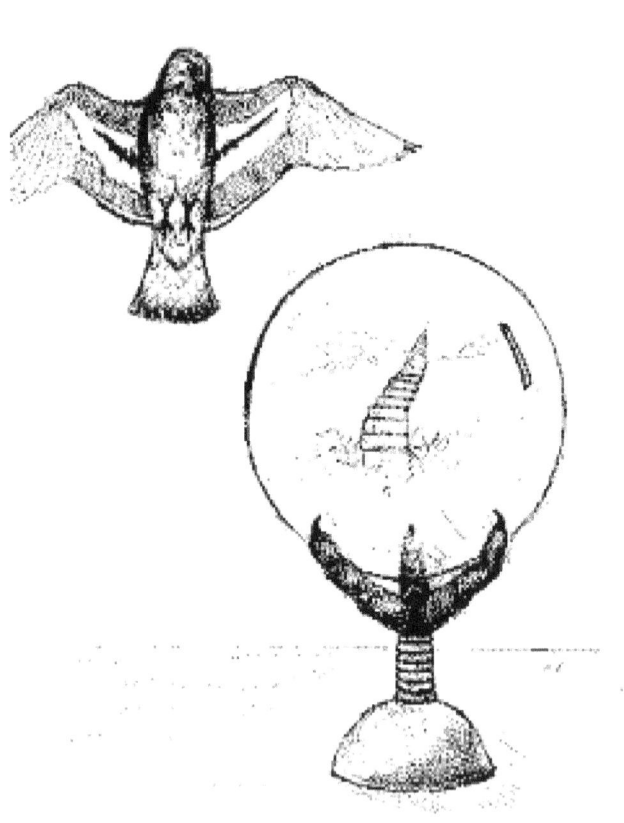

The best way to get results initially is to be in a dimly lit room. In this way nothing external will reflect off the crystal ball or crystal to misguide you. Place a black cloth underneath the crystal, or any stand it may be resting on, as this will also help to block out reflective light sources. Try to make your surroundings as quiet and peaceful as possible. In the beginning try working with the crystal alone. The least amount of distraction the better.

Now, look at the crystal and try to unfocus your gaze much as when you have been reading too long at one time. After a while you will start to see things. Most students expect to see very clear images and automatically understand everything they see right from the very start. This is seldom the case. Crystal gazing takes a lot of patience, but the results can certainly be very rewarding.

Sometimes the things you see in the crystal can be taken literally, other times your visions will be symbolic. You must learn to differentiate through experience. Sometimes you will see an image much as if you were watching a small TV set. There will be people in motion usually depicting future situations. As long as you maintain contact, the scene will continue. Other psychics

SECRET MAGICAL ELIXIRS OF LIFE

I know insist the crystal is really just a focal point for them, that the images are really in their head and not in the crystal at all.

One man I know saw himself on a boat out at sea. He felt it was somehow business connected. Next to him he saw a tall blond man who had a very large and very insincere smile on his face. The man was holding a stack of legal looking papers and was pointing a pen towards the person gazing into the crystal.

After the vision ended my acquaintance admitted he was puzzled as he did not understand how what he saw could possibly be applied to him. For one thing, he didn't even know anybody who owned a boat. Nor, for that matter, was he particularly fond of water. He proceeded, however, to make a note of the vision in a diary he kept for just such a purpose.

A few months went by and he had almost forgotten about the entire episode when he was called upon by a stranger at work.

The stranger was a blond man who had a profitable looking business proposition concerning ownership of a small fleet of fishing boats. It all seemed to come together at this point, and being more cautious then he normally would be, he found many inconsistencies and avoided making a bad business decision.

It's safe to say that some information comes in abstract, metaphysical terms. These are sometimes hard for the beginner to comprehend, whereas a psychic would be used to this type of data and would find it easier to understand. For example, sometimes images come in colors. Red would indicate intense emotions, pain and so forth. Other times there may be images of numbers and these may be related to numerology.

Two more ways for information to strike your senses would be through "feelings" and "hearing". Psychically you might feel a warmth, or a tingling sensation, or a glow that would indicate to you that something was going to transpire soon. Other times, you will verbally "hear" things of importance. This is really the clearest way to receive information. You may even turn around and answer someone before you realize you are alone.

You can also see the picture in black and white or in color. To see it in black and white does not mean you are not doing it right. The point is that you do get the information. If you receive the information in color, this is no guarantee that it will always come in this form. Your mind may switch back and forth.

Remember, it is not necessary to get information in a set way. The crystal is only a tool for your psychic input. While you are working with it you should try to keep all negativity from coming in your mind. You shouldn't be thinking about paying bills. It will work best for you when you have a sense of inner peace about you, perhaps a feeling of attunement with nature.

At the start don't try to rush matters. Work with you crystal for 15 or 20 minutes, otherwise you may become drained of all your psychic energy and you will end up blowing a mental fuse.

But whatever you do, remember to do it in good spirits and with a feeling of peace and tranquillity and before long you will be able to tune into yourself and others without any problem.

CHAPTER THREE

SELECTING THE PROPER STONE FOR YOU

Recently, we read a lot about crystals in the popular press, and while this is a good sign, the truth is that stones and gems of all types have their own purpose and reason for existing in the cosmic scheme of things. In this guide, I hope to cover the subject as extensively as possible, and provide information that is not readily available through most other sources.

Just as each individual has vibrational characteristics, so are there physical vibrations that come from stones themselves. Certain stones, such as quartz, can vibrate to your personal life force energy. Other stones may tune into you due to a particular experience or feeling you may be going through, such as hatred, greed, lust, joy, love, etc.

Stones can benefit everyone and they are even more helpful if they blend with your particular vibration.

Psychics are very sensitive to the vibrations of stones. They are able to tell you which particular stone is right for you. If you do not know a psychic or are not able to locate one, you can select your stones using the following procedure:

Place your hand over a number of varied stones. Run your hand with your palm facing downward back and forth across the stones, noting which ones have a warmer feeling to them. As you feel this, you should separate these stones from the rest. Then repeat the procedure until you cannot sense any more warmth coming from the remaining stones. Those that you have placed aside are to be your personal stones.

Once you begin to utilize these stones, do not let other people touch them. Because these stones are vibrating to you personally, you do not want them to be mixed with someone else's energies.

Your stones will begin to work for you after a period of time. However, realize that the power of the stones is not to replace the Divine Power, but rather to assist and to aid you as stepping stones, no pun intended.

SECRET MAGICAL ELIXIRS OF LIFE

HOW THE STONES WORK FOR YOU

Stones carry a physical vibration and act as a magnet. As a result, they attract other vibrations in their immediate vicinity. Thus, they are able to heighten one's sensitivity and send out their characteristic vibrations which affect and/or influence other physical bodies or the environment in its vicinity.

Each stone carries a particular vibration that attracts certain forces to it. These forces can manifest themselves as love, peace, money, protection, good luck, etc. For stones to work properly, they need to be carried within three feet of the individual they belong to. Otherwise, those things which you wish to attract will go to the closest person to the stones.

You may carry stones in your pocket, pocketbook, small bags, etc. You may also wear them as jewelry, amulets or talismans. When you want or need certain things in your life, you can simply look up the appropriate stones and utilize them. Whatever you can conceive of you can find a stone to do the job for you.

There is a mineral called Staruolite, or Baseler Taufstein, or Baptismal-Stone which is best know for its use as an amulet at Baptism rites. It has also been called a Fairy Cross. Though they are natural stones, they take on the shape of a cross. They have been formed in this way by nature and are thought to be a very good charm. There are many stories associated with this stone and why it is shaped the way it is. One such story tells of fairies playing by a spring when a messenger elf comes by to tell them about the crucifixion of Christ. The fairies become sad and start to cry and as their tears fall the tears turn into crosses.

By picking the proper stone it is possible to attract to you almost anything you concentrate upon. All you have to do is select the stone that aligns itself to your needs.

A few years back my television set just about fell apart, refusing to run. The set was pretty old and it was hardly worth putting the money into fixing it. Because of my financial status at the moment I was unable to buy a new set and realized that some drastic action was needed.

I picked a stone from my private collection that I knew would be of help to me. I selected a piece of Turquoise and proceeded to hold it in my hand

and concentrate on my need. I did NOT concentrate on how the TV would come to me, but only on the result of my concentration.

For the next two weeks, I spent a good 15 or 20 minutes a day in visualization, thanking the Divine Power for its help, and then I would let the thought go. Within a short while I had not one but three TV's!

First, a friend of mine brought over his TV set because he said he was too busy with work to watch it anyway. Then I received a small TV as a gift. Next, my mother purchased a nice set for me for my birthday. At this point I had three televisions in the house, all coming without my having to buy one. In fact, each one was better then the last!

Another time I used pretty much the same method to get an iron since mine wouldn't heat up right. Within three days a friend brought one for me as a gift and then my son, Rick, came home on leave from the Navy and decided not to take his iron overseas when he left. Things really got out of hand when another friend said he had two irons and could I use one of them! By then, of course, I didn't need his, but still someone else remembered mine wasn't working and offered to lend another iron to me.

It worked the same way when I told the Divine Power I was in desperate need of a typewriter on which to do my mail readings. Before long, I ended up with five typewriters.

Eventually, I had to hold a garage sale in order to clear out all the extra stuff I had managed to accumulate.

So, as you can tell, its not profitable to laugh and snicker at the benefits that can be derived from using the magickal vibrations to be found within stones and gems. After all, it might come to the point where they could help furnish your entire house!

SECRET MAGICAL ELIXIRS OF LIFE

STONES AND THEIR INDIVIDUAL USES

In using stones in your work please remember that they can be used either for positive or negative purposes. It all depends upon the situation because the Divine Forces are neutral - they are neither good nor bad. It is the person who utilizes the power that makes the stones work either way. You need to work with the positive to keep a positive flow moving, so that the more good you do the more good will come back to you.

Stones can be worn, carried, or placed in a room. For best results consult the information chart below which tells you the best purpose for the individual stones.

Agate Shields against evil spells. Attracts love and good luck. Black agate increases prosperity, and represents victory over all odds. Brown agate helps with money and provides a longer, more joyful life. Red agate has curative power, and is good for persons who were under the signs of Aries and Aquarius.

Lapis Lazuli Attracts strong spirits to you. Supernatural powers are said to be contained within the stone. Ranges in color from blue-violet to greenish blue and is often found within limestone. Is particularly beneficial to Sagittarius people.

Garnet This stone attracts sincerity, purity and logic on the mental level and should be used by those who are Aquarians or who were born under the sign of Capricorn.

Diamond There is no evidence that women live longer then men because they more often wear diamonds, which are very beneficial to one's ongoing health and energy supply. This is a good stone to bring about peace and fidelity between lovers and friends that have been fighting. Especially good for Aries and Leo.

Crystal When you wear a crystal you will have influence and power over others and over situations. Prevents bad dreams and protects from the evil eye, as well as being useful in a lot of other ways as indicated throughout this book.

Tigers Eye Brings good luck and protects against the evil eye.

Amethyst Protects against being drunk. Brings luck in life. Protects from black magick or evil spells. Produces intelligence and wisdom.

Bloodstone Offers success in court, wealth, soothing to people with bad tempers. Attracts friends. Protects from evil eye and depression. When held next to an area that is bleeding it stops the flow of blood. Good for Pisces, Scorpio and Virgo.

SECRET MAGICAL ELIXIRS OF LIFE

Jade Wear or carry for health reasons, especially for the person who has trouble in the area of the kidney. Protects against evil thoughts. Fights nightmares.

Carnelian Promotes courage. Calms the nerves. Defends against negativity.

Moonstone Brings lovers together. Enhances psychic powers. Attracts wisdom and wealth. For a person whose sign is Cancer, it can be used as an enhancer of serious passions. When worn around the neck it keeps away evil.

Crazy Lace Higher spirituality. Grace. Peace. Love. Harmony.

Beryl Protects from negative spells. Overcomes lazy attitudes. A round stone, if exposed to the sun, will kindle emotional fires.

Emerald Used for magickal purposes. It can turn curses and hexes back upon the sender. Beauty. Love. For Cancer, Gemini and Taurus.

Coral One of the strongest stones. Used against natural disasters, accidents, negativity. It is said that it changes color when one is near someone who is about to die. Good for Libra, Sagittarius and Taurus.

Onyx Breaks up romances and fosters arguments with others. Causes bad dreams.

Opal Dangerous for those not in harmony with the vibration of this stone. Any person who gets uneasy feelings from this stone should not wear it. A very mystical stone. Good for Cancer, Libra, and Scorpio.

Turquoise Helps take away tension. Brings protection. Love. Courage. Good for Libra, and Taurus.

Sardonyx Helps with accuracy. Adds warmth to a relationship. Wards off negativity. Leo and Virgo would be benefited.

Moss Agate Health. Happiness. Wealth. A very powerful stone.

Rose Quartz Health. Protection. Universal Love.

Jasper Finances. Draws money. Brings about good health in many cases.

SECRET MAGICAL ELIXIRS OF LIFE

CHAPTER FOUR

STONES AS TALISMAN

Let us start off this chapter by explaining exactly what a talisman is.

A talisman is an object that gives the wearer exceptional power. Throughout history talismans have often been used in performing ritualistic magick, or in helping the wearer to acquire the necessary energy to perform a spell. Most often, the power and energy is based upon the form and the shape of the particular talisman.

In the past, talismans were utilized to represent the elements: earth, wind, fire and water. They also represented God, the Saints or entities whose powers were to be used for help.

While belief in the power of a talisman may make it work all the better, belief is not really necessary for it to work. If you are wearing a talisman of protection and you do not believe in it, it will still work for you due to the vibration it puts out. However, if you fight against its power by disbelieving, it is as though you are being both positive and negative at the same time.

SECRET MAGICAL ELIXIRS OF LIFE

Talismanic stones are worn next to the skin when the use is medicinal. The stones can be hung from around your neck or worn on your wrist. Certain stones should be worn on specific parts of the body to bring out the right influences or energies. The main concern is the need to have body contact with the vibration of the talisman.

Because many believe the talisman needs to have body contact, the stones are often immersed in water to pass on their power. This is primarily used for medicinal purposes.

In the days of Camelot, the stones were put into a goblet, insuring that whatever liquid—be it water or wine—was in the goblet, also picked up the talisman's properties, and when drank would result in that person being psychically charged.

SECRET MAGICAL ELIXIRS OF LIFE
IMPORTANCE OF A STONE'S SHAPE

The shape is also important in a stone's use. Some shapes contain or transmit energy. One such shape is the pyramid. When you read books on pyramid power, you realize how much knowledge was actually known in the past. It has been scientifically proven that razor blades stay sharper inside the pyramid when properly aligned North to South. Food can also be preserved for a much longer period, and meat is kept fresher in exactly the same way. Plants grow better when kept under a pyramid. If a pyramid is placed over a bed, the sleeper regains his health faster, and sleeps better. Also, the energy flowing through that person will help to energize them while they are sleeping. Even hospitals are now using the shape of the pyramid in healing patients.

This is one of the reasons why diamonds and crystals that are cut in the shape of a pyramid are considered to be extra powerful or beneficial. If you look at a terminated clear quartz crystal some have tiny pyramids etched inside by nature. When you find one, you can program it to store memory. It is as though you have a small memory bank. When you want the information you merely retrieve it from your crystal. You hold the crystal in your hand when you are ready to program it, and then you concentrate on what information you want to store in it, finally blowing your intentions into the crystal for safe keeping.

Stones have great power by themselves. When contained in brooches or rings the power is often strengthened. The inscriptions may concentrate on heightening one of the powers of the stone, rather then giving it multiple benefits. For example, there are 99 names for God in Mohammedism alone and 10 in the Kabala. The intention may be written obviously, such as..."Those who wear this stone are protected from evil by night." Or they can be inscribed in the signs and symbols of the Magi, the Angelic alphabet, or some other "code" known only to the wearer. Many magicians and those who practice specific forms of occultism have noted that talisman rings can be used to attract the characteristic influences of specific planets. When you use the stones in this way you are using them as if they were magnets capable of bringing in the particular vibration that you wish. In short, when you combine the knowledge of the stone with other influences in your life, it makes a big difference. You are adding more power to that which you are working

SECRET MAGICAL ELIXIRS OF LIFE

on attracting toward you.

One of the characteristic influences of the stone is its alignment with activities of the planets in the heavens. You should try to combine planetary influences with the particular stones you are wearing.

The following table should serve as a list of the planets and what stones they have influence over:

PLANET	STONE	INFLUENCE
Sun	Diamond or Topaz in gold setting.	Obtaining wealth, making friends, gaining influences.
Moon	Pearl, Crystal or Quartz in silver.	Travel, love, messages.
Mercury	Opal or Agate in quicksilver.	Business, divination, controlling spirits.
Venus	Emerald or Turquoise in copper.	Making friends, traveling.
Mars	Ruby; any red color stone in iron.	Summoning souls.
Jupiter	Sapphire, Amethyst, Carnelian in tin.	Maintaining health, gaining riches, or honors.
Saturn	Onyx or Sapphire in lead.	Causing good or bad fortune, gaining possessions; destruction, discord

SECRET MAGICAL ELIXIRS OF LIFE

BRIDAL RINGS

There are many different stones that are a part of a bridal ring. Many associate the wedding ring with diamonds, but it was not always so, and there are still many who prefer another type of stone. In a bridal ring, these stones take on a more personal meaning as you can see from the specially prepared chart below:

TONE	MEANING
Amethyst	Unrelenting love
Opal	Hopefulness
Carnelian	Patience
Diamond	Virtue
Beryl	Mutual love
Emerald	Marital stability
Lodestone	Persuasion
Pearl	Chastity/Purity
Sapphire	Faith
Agate	Long Life/Health

NOTES

CHAPTER FIVE

HIDDEN MEANING OF STONES

There are a lot of things about stones that are, at least on the surface, hidden from us. This section attempts to clarify some of these areas and will hopefully enhance your appreciation of stones and gems as being more than just beautiful adornments.

As an example, have you ever noticed that when you buy jewelry for a loved one or a friend that there are certain stones which you will be attracted to in the jewelry case almost right off the bat? If you want to buy a ring for a friend, what colors or stones come to your mind? You will not always think of the same answer, when thinking of different friends.

Stones, you see, express certain sentiments. When you give or receive a gift of a stone always be certain to look for its hidden meaning. The chart below will give you a hand!

SECRET MAGICAL ELIXIRS OF LIFE

STONE	MEANING
Fire Opal	Adversity cannot defeat you
Moss Opal	Approval of you
Opal	Humility
Tiger Eye	Danger
Diamond	Joy, Happy Life, Attachment
Ruby	Success, Divine Strength, Power, Charitable Love
Balas Ruby	Domestic bliss
Sapphire	Faith, Hope, Affability
Bloodstone	Courage, Strength
Onyx	Marital Love, Devotion
Topaz	Faithfulness, Friendship
Bohemian Topaz	Fidelity in love or marriage
Emerald	Friendship is desired, Faithfulness
Carnelian	Friendship is offered, Leadership
Turquoise	Success and Good Fortune
Coral	Safety
Pearl	Humility, I am innocent attitude
Garnet	Trust in love

When someone of the opposite sex gives you a moonstone it will bind the two of you together and you both will have a connection on a spiritual level.

If you give or receive a Lapis, Ruby, Carnelian or any of the yellow gemstones, these stones are meant to help in uncrossing; that is, sending back negative forces.

Keep an eye out for what stone you receive and you will be more aware of how the giver of the gift feels towards you even though they may not consciously be aware of their true feelings.

SECRET MAGICAL ELIXIRS OF LIFE

There are times when you need to wear a certain stone more than others. This is due to the fact that you are going through a period when the vibrations of that stone are more needed in your life.

When you start to think in terms of meaning, you will also chose gifts with more discretion, and with more hidden significance.

COLOR OF THE STONES

The color of a stone can also play a role in strengthening the stone's natural powers and influences. The following is a chart delineating the various stones and colors and their meanings.

COLOR	MEANING
White	For friendship. Also a symbol for purity, religion.(Pearl)
Yellow	Represents secrecy. The sign of generosity. Ages ago it was a sign of nobility.(Jacinth)
Green	An aid to strengthen sight. This color in a stone is said to have curative powers. Stands for hope.(Emerald)
Blue	Houses the meaning of wisdom.(Sapphire)
Red	Represents passion. Controls the flow of blood—either to stop or cause.(Bloodstone)
Violet	Draws in spirituality. Also has a calming effect.(Sapphire)
Black	Control of envy. Deals with negativity. Has negative or positive power determined by its user.(Apache Tear)
Colorless	To protect the wearer from evil, or to send out negative influences.(Diamond)

SECRET MAGICAL ELIXIRS OF LIFE

BIRTHSTONES

There is more than one property to each stone. Some attract wealth, power or money, while others attract healing, meditation and psychic forces. Stones vibrate on more than one level. This is the reason why down through the ages, when someone needed wealth or power, they went to the stones for assistance.

Another advantage in using stones is that other people are not aware when you are working with them. They only look at them as ornaments, or if the stones are being carried, no one needs to be aware of it. You must remember not to let any other person touch your stone once you are utilizing it in this regard as it will lessen the vibrations that will be working on your behalf.

Birthstones have always been of importance and occultists have known about their use for thousands of years. The following will tell you what your birthstone is and what it represents. It is a natural talisman or amulet, certainly among the most powerful you will ever find.

SECRET MAGICAL ELIXIRS OF LIFE

MONTH	BIRTHSTONE	PURPOSE
January	Garnet	Symbol of stability and firmness.
February	Amethyst	Sincerity.
March	Bloodstone	Courage (Jasper for health/love).
April	Diamond	Chastity and purity.
May	Emerald	Success in affairs of the heart.
June	Agate	Long life and health.
July	Carnelian/Ruby	Contentment (or Onyx for luck).
August	Sardonyx	Marital bliss.
September	Sapphire	Strength.
October	Opal	Good luck and optimism.
November	Topaz	Love, friendship and fidelity.
December	Turquoise	Prosperity (or Ruby for success).

SECRET MAGICAL ELIXIRS OF LIFE

ASTROLOGICAL STONES

Those who study the position of the planets will already know the importance of stones and gems used according to their astrological influences. Regardless of what your sign may be, there are certain stones that will have a positive effect on you as long as you wear them. The following list takes you through the twelve signs of the zodiac.

ASTROLOGICAL SIGN TO WEAR OR CARRY	STONES OR GEMS
Aquarius	Garnet. Jade. Amazonite. Pyrite.
Pisces	Amethyst. Diamond. Zircon. Opal.
Aries	Bloodstone. Red Coral. Jasper. Carbuncle. Carnelian.
Taurus	Sapphire. Lapis Lazuli. Turquoise.
Gemini	Topaz. Amber. Emerald. Obsidian.
Cancer	Amethyst. Hematite.
Leo	Jasper. Agate. Pearl. Serpentine.
Virgo	Topaz. Amber. Obsidian.
Libra	Lapis Lazuli. Sapphire. Sodalite.
Scorpio	Ruby. Red Coral. Carnelian.
Sagittarius	Rock Crystal. Diamond. Opal.
Capricorn	Pyrite. Peridot. Malachite. Jade. Emerald.

SECRET MAGICAL ELIXIRS OF LIFE

NOTES

CHAPTER SIX

GEM ELIXIRS AND HEALTH STONES

There is an ancient belief which says that gems and stones can influence and improve your health.

When you use gem stones for medicine, it is called a "Gem Elixir." To get the desired effect you place the stone in a bowl of water, then you use the sun's vibrations by leaving the water outdoors all day and overnight. The mineral properties will be collected in the water for health or spiritual development. Remove the stone and simply drink the water to feel its effect.

Many times, the shape will also have a positive effect. We have already discussed the pyramid shaped stone and what it can do in other areas, and it is especially good for cleansing and healing. This particular shape promotes strength, healing and preserves psychic and high abilities. Many of the gemstones have the pyramid shape within them such as diamonds, and crystals. Both also have physical properties that aid in healing.

One of the best known talismans that utilizes stones is called Aaron's Breastplate which is discussed in Exodus 28:17. The Bible says, "And thou

SECRET MAGICAL ELIXIRS OF LIFE

shall set in it settings of stones, even four rows of stones: the first row shall be a ruby, a topaz and a garnet; in the second row, an emerald, a sapphire, and a diamond; in the third row, a turquoise, an agate, and an amethyst; and in the fourth row, a beryl, a carnelian, and a jasper. These are to be mounted in gold settings."

The stones themselves can have multifaceted powers. Stones are also utilized in rings, pendants, goblets, and also as carved images. The power is very strong in Aaron's Breastplate because of the combination of stones. Millions have seen this plate demonstrated in the film THE ARK OF THE COVENANT, and will at once realize the potential power it is said to have had.

SECRET MAGICAL ELIXIRS OF LIFE

THE POWER OF HEALING STONES

Though the author can make no claims for the ability for stones to heal or otherwise cure ailments, wisemen throughout the ages have used them for such a purpose. And while you should always consult a qualified physician the moment you are not feeling well, it certainly wouldn't hurt to carry your favorite stone along with you whenever you feel it might help wipe away your blues or put you into a better frame of mind.

The chart that follows is an accurate representation of the various stones and what they are believed capable of doing in the area of health and healing, as well as in general.

It should serve as a handy reference for all those who believe in the holistic principles that are so widely being adopted today by people from all walks of life. And in addition it should be of widespread use to those who are looking for a source to tell them the all around purpose of stones in various categories.

STONE	PURPOSE
Agate	Helps to strengthen eyesight. If held in a sick person's hand it helps speed the healing. Moss Agate helps to have a good harvest if worn on the upper right arm of a man or a women.
Ruby	It is considered lucky to wear it on the left side of the body. Helps concentrate mentally. Wear so as not to fear your enemies.
Moonstone	To gain knowledge, place it in your mouth when the moon is waning and pray to Gabriel for help through Divine Power. To free yourself of a failing heart due to a poor romance, place the stone in your mouth while the moon is full.

SECRET MAGICAL ELIXIRS OF LIFE

Lapis Lazuli Psychic attunement. To be in tune with higher consciousness. Strengthens the body. Self-assurance can be improved.

Opal Stops anger. Held in the left hand and concentrated upon it will bring your desires to a reality level.

Sapphire Attracts Divine favor. Has power to influence spirits. Can help to communicate with a person who has passed on.

Jasper Brings about general good health. One of the best and strongest stones for this purpose. Also protects from evil spirits.

Jade If worn around the neck of children it will protect them from ailment.

Topaz Takes away night fears. Heightens intelligence.

Azurite Changes mental thoughts and vibrations. Helps to gain mental balance. Opens 3rd Eye. Invokes spirits help and puts you in tune with the astral plane.

Peridot Worn to take away fears, guilt, depressed mood.

Amethyst Highest vibration for 3rd Eye Chakra. Placed over the 3rd Eye it helps in meditation. For passion, hope, truth, and love.

Bloodstone Used as an amulet to protect against the evil eye.

Tektite Known to be extraterrestrial in origin. Increases psychic ability. Balances.

SECRET MAGICAL ELIXIRS OF LIFE

Tourmaline Regenerates and protects. Helps to release negativity.

Apache Tear Cleanses. Elevates psychic ability. Draws energy to the sexual organs.

Fluorite Acts as a catalyst. Good for study aid. Higher mental levels. Ground excess energy. Truth and positive outlook.

Black Obsidian Master Teacher. Takes away illusions and clears up negativity.

Herkimer Starts inner changes. Unlocks potentials.

Diamond Good for mediumistic work. Brings about lucid dreams.

Rhodochrosite Very strong love stone. Helps others to understand you when speaking or passing on information. Ideal for anyone who has to deal with the public.

CHAPTER SEVEN

MAGICKAL STONES TO HELP CAST A BLESSING

Stones have always served as a part of occult magick. The first cave man to look at a stone polished by the running river, and seeing "fire" in it from the sun, surely must have thought that the stone was magickal.

A basis for many ancient religions, stones were considered to be very special by the Druids who utilized places like Stonehenge in England for their religious rites. In actuality, the Druids were not the first to hold rituals on Salisbury Plain. Stonehenge had already been in use for this very purpose for more than a thousand years by other lesser known groups who sensed the importance of these standing stones. The truth is that the Druids did tear down some of the original blocks of stones and erected some much larger rocks-some weighing as much as 40 tons. They apparently dragged these massive blocks from as far as Wales, thus bypassing many local stones. The reason for this is that apparently the blocks they brought in from the greater distance contained a certain element-natural quartz crystal-which

SECRET MAGICAL ELIXIRS OF LIFE

made their magickal rituals even more potent than they might otherwise have been.

Upon moving, many early cultures would take their magickal stones with them no matter how large or how many stones might already exist in the region they were moving to. Stones were considered sacred and were used as protection against the new environment. Also, this was a method used by some to take the spirits of relatives that had passed on with them.

Any time you work with magick you are working with the laws of nature. If you know how to work with these energies the magick you perform will be very powerful. There is, after all, power, energy, and force in all stones.

SECRET MAGICAL ELIXIRS OF LIFE

EARTH MAGICK

The type of magick we have just described is most commonly referred to as "Earth Magick," representing a form of casting spells that is generally accepted as being thousands of years old. When you are working with Earth Magick there are some important things to remember:

1. Magick is natural. You are working with nature to make changes in your life or in someone else's life. It has been used through the ages. We are just as much a part of nature as the stones, earth, water, air and all life forms.

2. We never harm anyone. Remember that negativity always comes back to haunt the sender.

3. Magick is serious business. You should never undertake such a venture lightly.

4. You should be knowledgeable. You have to be certain about what you are doing. You do not want to get hurt, or get results you did not expect.

5. Work ONLY positive magick. Working through Divine Power is a major rule.

6. Keep at what you're doing. You shouldn't expect success to necessarily come over night (although sometimes it does).

7. Visualize. You need a strong ability to visualize to help get things going.

8. The main ingredient in making any spell work is WILL POWER.

You need to work with total conviction and utter sincerity. Do not attempt to do too many things at one time as it is better to concentrate your thoughts and actions on one spell and not several. And, if you are doing magick for others, always do it for yourself last.

SECRET MAGICAL ELIXIRS OF LIFE
GEMS AND THEIR RELATED HOURS

The best times to start using the stones if possible are as follows:

GEM	DAY HOUR	GEM	NIGHT HOUR
Chrysolite	7am	**Sardonyx**	7pm
Amethyst	8am	**Chalcedony**	8pm
Kunzite	9am	**Jade**	9pm
Sapphire	10am	**Jasper**	10pm
Garnet	11am	**Lodestone**	11pm
Diamond	Noon	**Onyx**	Midnight
Jacinth	1pm	**Morion**	1am
Emerald	2pm	**Hematite**	2am
Beryl	3pm	**Malachite**	3am
Topaz	4pm	**Lapis Lazuli**	4am
Ruby	5pm	**Turquoise**	5am
Opal	6pm	**Tourmaline**	6am

Timing can be very important in performing magick. Try to start at the right hour by looking up the correct day on the chart that contains planets and their influences. It is easier when you are working with stones since even if you do not correlate the proper times, the stones themselves have a magnetic force and will work. However, if you do use this scale, you are making your spell all the stronger.

Visualization is very important. After all, if you can't see what you want in your mind, how are you going to attract it to you? Stop for a minute and think of a person you love, or a pet, or even your car. As soon as you think of them, you immediately form a picture in your mind. This is visualization. It focuses your desire and points the energy in the right direction. You are deliberately choosing and working on a definite result.

Visualize yourself as already having what you desire. If you want a relationship, picture yourself watching a movie together, or whatever you would like to do. If you are working on a material desire, visualize yourself already using it. As an example, if you want a car, picture yourself driving that automobile.

Give thanks to God for this or something better, and for the good of all. This sets your subconscious to expect the result.

Next, let go of your desire. Do other things, and do not put more time or effort into it. Every now and then, you can reaffirm, but not too frequently, since that causes doubt that it is working. You are now leaving it in God's hands. He wants us to be happy in all phases of our lives. In the Bible in Matt.7:7 it says, "Ask and it shall be given you, seek, and ye shall find, knock, and it shall be opened unto you." The Bible does not say "maybe," it says "shall." In essence, what you expect from life will be what you get. Expect good. Expect your desire to be fulfilled. The Bible says, Matt.9:29, "According to your faith be it unto you." You only need to remember when you are working with the stones that GOD DOES NOT MAKE MISTAKES!

Another important step to remember is not to tell others what you are doing. Only those who would support your goals. You may tell a person who does not understand, or is of a negative nature. This means you would have negativity sent towards you. You may then subconsciously accept their negativity, and thus cause a delay in the results you want. It is best to keep it a secret while you are working towards a goal.

Also remember that what you want may come in an unexpected way. So you need to work with it. As an example, you are looking for a new job. You hold the stone in your hand, and go through the rest of the magick steps. You are walking down the street one sunny day, and you are in a hurry to go to a specific store. Suddenly you have an urge to go down an unfamiliar street to get there. Normally, you would ignore the urge. However, you realize that you are working towards a goal, and it may come in an unusual way. It is sunny and warm. The worst that can happen is that you arrived from a different direction. So you are now walking in this new direction, and you happen to run into an old friend that you have not seen in ages. You start talking about how things are going for both of you, and your friend learns of your search for a better job. Your friend then tells you of an opening for just the type of job you would like in an office nearby. It just opened and others do not even know it yet. So, forgetting about the store for now, you go and apply and get the job. All this, simply because you were working with the stones and listened to your inner urgings. See how easily it works?

When you work with the stones and also do your part in acting on your inner feelings and ideas, unexpected doors will open up for you. At times, you have fall-out. This means that when you are working on a particular desire, you may also have another one come in, that you were not even concentrating on.

Now that you are aware of what you are dealing with and how to work with it, it is time to put this power to use.

EARTH AND WATER SPELL

You hold the stone in your passive hand (that would be the hand that you do not write with). Put all your desires and concentration into the stone. Feel them going into it. Then take the stone to a running river or stream and throw it in. Or bury the stone where it will not be disturbed. Go home and forget about it. The results will come to you.

PROTECTION

Mix 1 teaspoon (or a little more) of sea salt in 1 cup of water. Add to this four quartz crystals and leave it in direct sunlight for three days. On the fourth day, take the stones out and place them in the four corners of the room that you need the protection in. This will also cleanse a house and keep negative spirits away. Positive ones are not kept out.

WHEN BUSINESS IS BAD

Take a Bloodstone and a Jasper and put them into the back of your cash register. Also, take the same type of stones and concentrate on your needs, breathe on them, then put them into a pouch or bag that is of a green color. You need to carry this with you at all times. Do not let anyone else touch the bag, and do not discuss what you are working on.

PURIFICATION BATH

Put sea salt and Crazy Lace, Amethyst, Tiger Eye, and Rose Quartz into your bath water. Soak for 10-20 minutes. This is not for a bath, only for purification, and should be used only as such. Baths change the personal vibrations due to their properties.

Water is a symbol of life and has the ability to purify.

After any bath, let your body air dry.

PSYCHIC INFORMATION OR FOR INFORMATION ABOUT A PERSON

You need to place a Herkimer Diamond under your pillow at night before going to sleep. Concentrate on the question you would like to ask, or the information you would like to receive. Think of nothing else. Make it the last thing that goes through your mind at night, then go to sleep. When you wake up, make a note of everything you dreamt. Your dreams will become very clear and vivid. The information will come to you in this manner and you should get your answer within three nights.

LOVE SPELL

Soak a Moonstone for an hour in a glass of water that you have placed where the sun will shine on it. Then place the glass in the refrigerator. When the person you desire comes over, remove the stone and have them drink the water. Also give the person a Moonstone wrapped in yellow silk as a gift. This will tie you both together.

SECRET MAGICAL ELIXIRS OF LIFE

MONEY DRAWING

Light a green candle measuring about 7 inches tall. Hold a piece of Jasper in your passive hand. Concentrate on money coming to you in the amount needed and more, through Divine Power, and in a perfect way. Then say: As the Light in front of me, I also have Divine Power shining through me. As everything comes from above, so now money comes also, enough and to spare, to this material level, as the stone before came into being from Divine Power. Thank you Lord. So be it.

Repeat this for 5 minutes a night, for 7 nights in a row.

LOVE ATTRACTION

Write the name of the one you love in red on a Moonstone or any one of the stones used for love. Then next to it, write your own name. Do not use any capital letters in the names. Repeat this 7 times and concentrate for 5 minutes on what you want. Then carefully wrap the stone in an elm leaf with some Lavender mixed with it. You then bury this in your yard or in a flower pot in your home. Leave it there and forget about it.

FOR GOOD LUCK

In an orange bag mix the following: A Jade stone, Apache Tears (you need three) and Sodalite. Also add the herbs: linden, grains of paradise, star anise and snakeroot. Do not let anyone see it and carry this "Good Luck" bag with you at all times.

TO HELP IN MEDITATION

Make sure you are in a comfortable chair. Relax, and before you follow your meditation steps, place a Herkimer Diamond near you as well as a Quartz Crystal. Also light a White Light so you are only dealing with positive energy.

They need to be within 3 feet to work. However, you can hold them in your hand if you prefer.

FOR WEALTH

In a green bag, and in four corners of your home, you need to place the following mixture: Moss Agate, Moonstone, and Bloodstone. Mix them with the herbs called alfalfa, fenugreek, 2 tonka beans and chamomile. Carry the bag with you when you leave the house, and make sure the blend you place in the house is not in sight. You do not want questions. The blend does not need to be in sight, only in the corners, not sealed in anything tight.

THE PROSPERITY SPELL

Mix together the following herbs in something that you can burn them in: alfalfa, oak and, vervain. Make the herbs into the shape of a nest and in the middle place a Bloodstone, a Turquoise and an Adventurine stone. Now light the herbs, and focus on prosperity coming your way. After all, you deserve it. When it goes out, relight it until most or all the herbs are burned. Gather the stones and ashes together and place them in an orange cloth. Wrap them up and bury them in your yard at night or in a flower pot in your home where they will not be touched.

When you are done, do not forget to thank God for the prosperity that is NOW yours.

HARMONY AROUND YOU

Place the following herbs around your house at the four corners of the compass (you can also plant them if you like). To the east, west, north and south; Lavender, pennyroyal, violet, and myrtle. Next, place the following four stones next to them: Amethyst, Carnelian, Sodalite and Moss Agate. Then say: As the balance of Mother Nature works in harmony, so do those who enter here. So be it.

When you use herbs, you need to replace them about every 6-8 months. Their strength diminishes with time.

TO STRENGTHEN SPIRITUALITY

Put the following into a purple bag: a Quartz Crystal, Crazy Lace, and a Moonstone. Add to this the herbs: sandalwood, myrrh (always use myrrh with the next herb), frankincense. After you have made the blend, before putting it into the bag, gently blow on it. Then tie the bag with 7 knots, and blow on it again. Also work with it consciously and do not do things in your life that are negative.

TO GRANT YOUR WISHES

To a bowl or container that would hold the contents for a length of time, add the following: Moss Agate, Turquoise, and Adventurine, the herbs called sage, 2 tonka beans, ginseng, and grains of paradise.

Every night at the same time, until your wish is granted, take the bowl out, and hold your receptive hand over it. Concentrate on your needs as you visualize what you want and add as much detail as you want. Remember not to think of HOW you are getting your wish, only of the end result. Do this for at least 5 minutes a day, or 5 times a day.

LOVE ATTRACTION

To attract the one you want into your life, do the next steps as outlined. First, obtain an object that is his (or her) personal possession, such as a piece of hair, or a thread of clothing. Next, get a Turquoise stone and wrap this object around it 7 times. Now mix the herbs: linden, lotus, chamomile, jasmine, clover, and rose. Put all the ingredients in a small bag and always carry it, especially when near that person.

MEDITATION

When you meditate, whatever method you may use, it can be enhanced by the stones. Place a Herkimer Diamond near to you or hold it in your hand. This stone is especially good if you are working on a psychic level, as it helps with Trance mediumship. Many mediums use this stone. Also have a clear quartz crystal near to you. This will cleanse the area, so you tune into positive information and Spirit. It will keep negativity away and I suggest the use of both.

TO BREAK A HEX

Every now and then, there are negative energies sent towards you, sometimes intentionally, sometimes not. However, even if someone is not working on this level in a negative way to send harm to you, you may receive the energy anyway. For example, if you have someone that is very jealous of you, they may wish that you not do well so strongly that you will receive the negativity.

You need to carry a Quartz Crystal with you at all times. Also, a Rose Quartz and an Apache Tear. You may wear them as jewelry, or carry them in a pouch. Also, cut out the form of a doll on black paper. Put this under your mattress and leave it there for 7 nights. You are very open on a psychic level when you are asleep. When you do this, the negative energies sent towards you will go through you, and into the doll. After 7 nights, burn the doll, and scatter the ashes to the winds. Make sure that you do not throw them out in your house. That is the same as holding on to it.

You may do this for a few weeks to make sure you are not sent the negativity, if you would like to. Make sure you change the doll every 7th night.

You are not doing anything negative. You are only sending back what has been sent to you. At times, you can actually see who is sending this to you. Your friend may get accident prone, or their car won't start when there isn't a reason for this to happen.

RITUAL TIMES

These are the best times, but if not convenient, the spells will work anyway.

New Moon To manifest something.

Waxing Moon (New moon to full moon.) To increase. Give vitality. To activate

Full Moon High energy point. Fulfillment, if work is done from full moon to now. Starting now—elimination.

Waning Moon (Full moon to new moon.) Banishing and decreasing work are to be done at this time.

CHAPTER EIGHT
LAPIS LAZULI
PSYCHIC POWER STONE

The Lapis Lazuli is known for being the oldest spirtual stone and has a high vibration on a psychic level. It is a crystalline stone of a bluish-green color and mentioned with frequency by Edgar Cayce in his trance states. Though there are two kinds, they both are powerful. The strongest is from Afghanistan.

This stone, when near you, will give you increased sensitivity and psychic awareness.

It is also used in meditation to assist in bringing you to the alpha state. Alpha has been scientifically tested as a brain wave level, a deeper level than our normal consciousness.

There are a number of dimensions and planes that coexist. When you are on a psychic level, you are tapping into the astral plane for your information. This is the level where occultists and psychics work. This is where spirits, angels, invisible beings, and thought forms reside. These co-existing planes are where you have your out-of-body (OOB) experiences known as astral projection.

During the 19th century more people consciously put their efforts into working on the astral plane. Drawing towards the Aquarian Age, we have more of an instinct toward the inner and outer knowledge.

Looking around you, you will see the start. More people will be utilizing the Lapis Lazuli, among other sources.

The Lapis was previously called Lapis Linguis. The stone's power comes in part from its crystal properties, but the Lapis taps into a higher frequency.

Used for any form of dowsing, this stone should be easy to get results with. Attached to any dowsing rod or pendulum, it should be highly sensitive.

When activated through meditation on this stone in conjunction with other elements connected to it, you are put in touch with the elemental spirits of this stone. This method of communication has been passed down for centuries through the higher occult cultures, such as Mu, Druids, etc. It has always been there. However, at times, due to the cultural outlook of that period, it was buried in secrecy. Its use was passed down through word of mouth, or in secret coded writings.

This stone was also revered for its healing strength. It focuses the energies from the other plane to this one. If the person with the health problem allows the healing energy to work, the normal healing process will be speeded up and thus they will be cured. If however, for some subconscious reason the person does not want to be helped, the healing energy will merely flow through and keep going.

One such man constantly had a headache every time he had to visit his in-laws. Now, the headache was very physically real. He did not want to go, but since he did not want to hurt his wife's feelings, his subconscious gave him an "out". The healing had absolutely no effect upon him. However, when he came to realize why and how to cope with the situation in a positive way, the healing took effect. Awareness also worked as a preventive measure for future headaches from the same cause.

The size does not make a difference in the stone, since we are dealing with its frequency level.

At times in your life, you may have a decision to make and not be able to focus. Then carry the Lapis Lazuli and it will heighten your mental ability as well as other levels. The decision will come to you much more smoothly.

When placed under your pillow, or near your bed, it makes you dreams become clearer.

Much like the quartz crystal, it heightens your own abilities when worn on your body, touching your skin. Whatever your known abilities may be, your true abilities may come as a suprise. You may think you are good with art, and your electronic abilities come in full force.

Connected with the throat chakra, it assists with anything associateded with that area. It makes you a more fluent speaker and is especially good if you are shy. It heals and cleanses anything dealing with the throat area, although it is diversified in other physical areas.

The Scarab used in Egypt contained the Lapis Lazuli. They were very well acquainted with its many uses. The design itself adds its own power and it was used by Egyptian royalty and considered valuable.

To charge the stone to its full strength, leave it under the full moon over night.

The best way to see how the Lapis Lazuli works is to try it on your own.

SECRET MAGICAL ELIXIRS OF LIFE

Carry the stone touching your skin-you can hang it on a chain. Do this for two weeks only taking it off when you are in the shower (it will not effect the stone, but it may effect your chain). Pay close attention to everything around you. After the two weeks, answer these questions:

- Were your dreams more vivid?
- In what way?
- What colors did you see more frequently?
- Example: Red-in cars, clothes, etc.
- What moods were more frequent?
- How was your health?

CHAPTER NINE
LUCID DREAMS

We can use stones to enhance the quality of our dreams.

Lucid dreams are more frequent than one might surmise. This is the experience of being conscious in a dream state.

Have you ever been aware that you are dreaming while you are in a dream state? Perhaps you are having a dream and suddenly you realize that you are not awake though it seems very real.

Such a state of awareness has not been prevalent in our society, but it is now starting to become more frequent. Many say it is due to our being on the brink of a new age. Others say we are getting more in tune, as we were in the past. Whatever the reason behind it, lucid dreams are more prevalent than before.

The subject suddenly is being discussed nation wide. You can read about it in books, magazines, see it on T.V., and even buy tapes discussing the subject.

There are people who have lucid dreams and would rather not know what is coming into their lives (their future). They do not want to consciously deal with it.

There are varied approaches to the dream state. They have been analyzed and looked at from a metephysical viewpoint ever since people realized they had dreams.

One approach is to interpret the dream. Freud used this method although he overdid it and looked at all dreams only from one angle. He felt that messages came from our subconscious mind and needed to be analyzed.

People using his method also feel that the person having the dream has only a small amount of decision in what happens inside the dream. Therefore, the dreamer is not responsible for whatever the dreams content is.

The newest and oldest way to look at it differs. It is thought to be the borderline between this world and the next. There are two parts: (1)The dreamer. (2)The content of the dream.

The dream content is considered the aspect of us that grows, that needs to be more than what we already are.

The dreamer has the control to stop the dream. However, the other option is to be aware it is a dream and flow with it consciously. See the conflicts inside the dream and go with it anyway. You know you are not really going to die if it is a negative dream. Interact with the Divine Light within yourself. You need to consciously respond in the dream in a positive way, to its conclusion.

As an example: You dream there is a dragon chasing you. You can either run, and thus make it a nightmare (negative), or you can consciously decide to change the response (positive). When the dragon chases you, turn around to face it, think of yourself as sitting cross legged on the ground as it comes towards you, and feel inner peace (or think of Divine Energy). You will find the dragon will either keep going past you, or stop and be friendly.

Then analyze what happened in the dream. How did you act within it?

In yoga, the lucid dream state is consciously worked toward. In The Book

SECRET MAGICAL ELIXIRS OF LIFE

of the Dead, it is made reference to. They say that upon leaving our reality to go into the dream state, you will see a bright light. They say this light pulls the soul towards its natural home. They feel people are asleep in our reality and that we all want to be one with the White Light again. Whether this is true or not, it does mean that people were intrigued with dreams and how to deal with them and their meanings since ancient times.

There are varied levels of lucid dreams.

Our normal sleep—with little activity occurring. Levels of dream state—light or mild. More intense—when you can ask for Divine Guidance and let go.

You can look at the dream and decide on how you want to solve it. This helps you deal with the world better (outside influences) and within yourself (internal or attitude changes).

If you go deeper, it is a trance state and you would see the White Light. Kundalini vibrates on this level.

You are NOT to change the dream; ONLY the way you respond within the dream itself. Counteract anything negative you encounter with Love. This is the strongest Universal Force.

To achieve the lucid dream state:

Before you go to sleep, place a Herkimer Diamond next to your bed(within 3 feet), or under your pillow. Affirm that you are going to have a lucid dream.

If you have a dream that keeps repeating, affirm the next time you have it that you will wake up in it and be aware. Reaffirm this several times.

Then meditate. It is said the best time is 5:30 - 8:00 a.m., or at the *same* time each night.

Practice every night and you will see the results, the changes within yourself and a more positive way of dealing with the world.

NOTES

CHAPTER TEN

PSYCHOMETRY WITH STONES

Psychometry is considered to be a science and an art. It is derived from the two Greek words, psyche (soul) and metron (measure). In this day, people think of it as a way of holding an object and picking up information from it on a psychic level.

Objects absorb magnetic vibrations into their aura from people and their surroundings. A psychic or someone who is sensitive to their vibrations can pick up this information. Psychometry is not limited to holding objects, however, that is our main concern at this time.

A gem stone or any stone can give you a fountain of knowledge. Hold the stone in your receptive hand.

Always go by your first intuitive feeling. (First hunch or gut feeling—it's the same.) The first will always be correct. The second feeling is from intellect or emotion. Neither is accurate. Trust the first, even when it seems impossible or does not make sense.

Try to analyze your feelings. Then practice expressing in words what

SECRET MAGICAL ELIXIRS OF LIFE

your impressions are.

Ask yourself *when*. Example: When will it occur? (Year, time, etc.) When will the next flood happen?

Ask *where*. Example: Where did it originate, or get lost?

Ask how. Example: How was it used? How did it happen?

When I work with the police or a detective, they may need to know how something was done.

Ask *who*. Example: Who did it? Ask for a name. In a theft, you can supply very useful information to locate the thief.

Ask *what*. Example: What is the object's use? What is the end result? What is in the area around the object?

Ask *why*. Example: Why did it happen? If you had a fire in your house, you would want to know the origin to prevent its repetition.

Holding a gem stone, you would find the area it came from. A friend of mine was holding a turquoise stone, and he kept feeling Native Americans near and the sensations of a Native American Indian drum. The stone turned out to be from an Indian reservation. You could pick up how people around it were dressed. What the climate was. Earthquakes—you would not pick that location to build your new home. Weather conditions can be of great use. There are numerous ways to utilize,

PSYCHOMETRY

When you need water on a farm, you can dowse for it, or you can check the stones to feel if there is water near or below the stone.

Try holding a gem stone that a friend has worn and see what your first impression is. You may be surprised!

CHAPTER ELEVEN

PREDICTING THE FUTURE

Diviners or soothsayers have always been with us. From earliest times, humankind has always had a fascination with what the future may hold. There are numerous methods that may be utilized to know what lies ahead.

Some people are psychic and "know" what is coming through clairvoyance (a knowing or seeing), or clairaudience (hearing), and a number of other ways, without the aid of any tools. They consciously tune into the Universal Mind for the information wanted.

Many people have the ability to communicate with one another on a psychic level. There are numerous cases of this already on record.

The ones we have heard of however, are sometimes extreme, such as when a parent "hears" a child cry out for help when the child is in trouble, and the parent gets there in the nick of time. The child, being at a distance, could not have been actually heard in the normal sense. This type of hearing is known as clairaudience.

Have you ever answered someone's question, and then realized that the person has not said anything? Or after you answer, the person says, "I was just going to ask you about that?" That is one form of psychic communication.

There are varied ways of communication on this level, some of which we are not aware of even though we may be psychic. At times, even the most intuitive people do not recognize what it is they are doing.

First impressions are a form of this. They are correct 100% of the time. It is only a matter of listening to your first intuitive feeling or hunch. The more you direct your life by it, the more frequent the feeling becomes. It has a snowball effect. There are numerous valid reasons to listen to your first impressions.

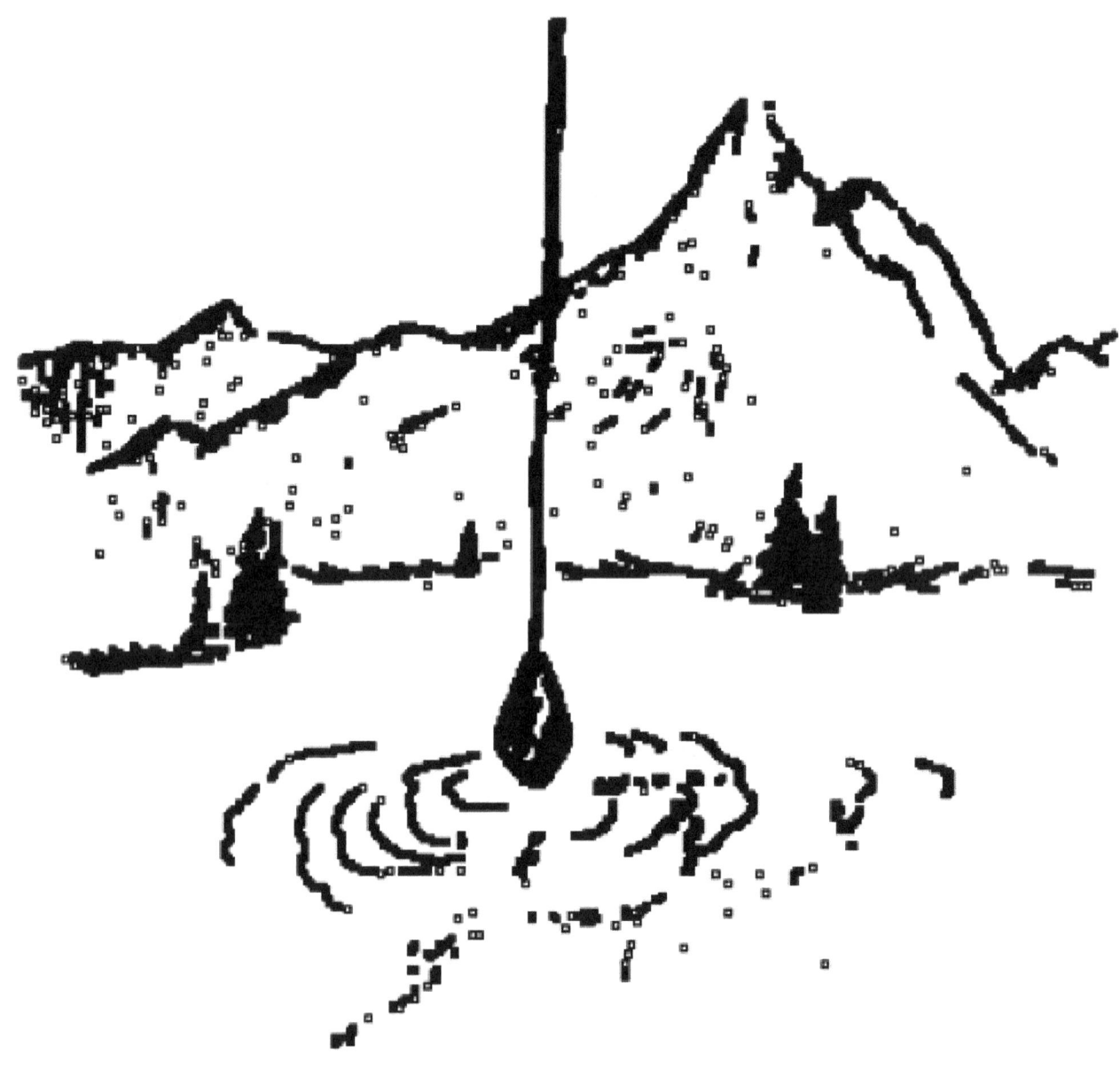

SECRET MAGICAL ELIXIRS OF LIFE

In the instance of meeting someone as a potential relationship or friendship, the person may be very warm and friendly, but if you still do not like the person, there is a reason. Later you will find that you do not get along on some level. Instead of trying harder to be friends—more out of guilt then any other reason—do not let it concern you. There are underlying reasons for the feeling. This is probably the type of person who acts like a friend, and the first time you need help, they are nowhere to be found. The reverse may also occur, as in getting a positive feeling about someone that outwardly seems negative. Learn to listen to your feelings more.

You may have a significant decision to make. Concentrate for 5 minutes on the decision. Look at all the aspects, both negative and positive. Then spend approximately 15 minutes sitting in silence by yourself. Do not think of anything negative, and do not think of anything related to the decision. Then, after the given time, think of the decision once again. The first feeling you receive will be your answer. For example, you are considering whether to move to Florida or Alaska. If your first feeling is one of warmth or palm trees, obviously you are not meant to be in Alaska.

The majority of people assume that there are only a few ways to receive psychic information. Thus, they miss their own abilities. They ignore the input they receive. A number of theories are recognized concerning varied psychic levels. One is that, in effect, we are all born with the ability and it manifests in different forms or levels. As previously mentioned, people intellectualize and try to understand. However, they do not take the most important step which is to apply this to themselves.

This source of information is for everyone. It comes to us from the astral plane. When we need information, we tune into the Universal Mind—the Akashic Records. We merely need to utilize it.

Another level of psychic communication is a "feeling." For example, when you are walking down the street and know if you turn around, there will be someone looking at you. Understanding this feeling as being correct may be of enormous help. It may even turn out to be a friend that you would have otherwise missed seeing. The principle of the psychic communication at work is to listen to the input and then utilize it.

There is a "knowing." This is displayed when you have an urge to stop in a store and then by "accident" run into a business contact, when previously you could not even get the person on the phone.

There are many contributing factors to what psychic communication means on a personal level. You need to trust your feelings, and then to act on them.

Man's culture has produced numerous responses on the psychic level. For example, working with spirits, herbs, gemstones, etc. was once widely accepted. There were more people working with this concept. If, in our society, it is considered "normal" and accepted, then we feel comfortable developing our psychic abilities. However, if you lived in Salem at the wrong time in history, then obviously, that was not the time to tell others you "knew" things they did not.

Animals have always sensed danger and run away before actually encountering the enemy. We must also have had the same ability on a higher level during the time when it was needed. There must have been some reason, besides intellect, for the cave man to have survived all the dangers they had to face.

Psychic communication has always been with us. It is merely a matter of our outlook.

Pay more attention to your feelings! Utilize them. Then your life will follow a smoother, happier path. Trust in yourself and in the source of your information - the Divine Power.

Others use tools to help them tune into a psychic level, such as the crystal ball, tarot, dowsing rod or rune stones.

The tools enable you to make a connection between this reality and the one on the astral plane. Both are just as real. It is as though you are walking on a thin line when you do anything psychic. On one side is reality and the other side is the astral. You can see both equally well. For example, in looking through a kaleidoscope, you turn it a little one way and see the astral levels, and when you turn it back, you refocus on this reality.

SECRET MAGICAL ELIXIRS OF LIFE
THE PENDULUM

The pendulum is one of the oldest psychic tools still in wide use to this day.

A pendulum is a small weight, (in this case one of your favorite stones) suspended from a chain or white string, preferably about 3" in length. For best results use Lapis, Rose Quartz or plain Quartz Crystal, though any stone that tends to be pointed will do fine.

First, hold the string or chain in the hand you use to write with. Hold it at the end between your thumb and index finger. The pendulum will move easily in this manner. Do not rest your elbow on anything.

Next, program the pendulum. You are using your subconscious to tune into the Universal Mind - your Source. There are only 5 directions for it to move: clockwise, counterclockwise, side to side, back and forth, or no movement at all (standstill).

Tell your pendulum you want it to move back and forth to mean YES (or clockwise), or side to side to mean NO (or counterclockwise).

Talk to your pendulum verbally to start. Ask it to show you YES, then NO with big swings.

In the beginning, ONLY ask questions to which you know the answers. You will get the knack of how to work with it. Also, do not go on to the next step until you get the correct answers ALL the time. You may need time for your subconscious to tune into the information for you.

Next, ask questions that are easy and to which you can get fast answers, such as: Am I _____ years old? Do not ask how much gold is in Fort Knox.

You can now ask questions that are more definite. Example: By how many points will the Karate Championship be won? 1-4?, 4-8?, etc.

Keep a log of how you have done. It is for visual feedback to indicate to you that the pendulum is working.

If you get slow answers, cup your hands around running water (sink). This gives the pendulum energy.

If you ask a question and it does not move, you are simply not meant to have an answer at that time. Do not rephrase it. Wait until the next day to try it again. Instead, go on to another question.

Pendulums are known to determine the sex of an unborn child. Hold it over the back of you hand (palm down), and ask your questions. It will go in a clockwise direction for a girl and counterclockwise for a boy. When it no longer moves, it is signifying there are no more children than already indicated.

Pendulums have been responsible for discovering missing persons, stonlen items, and land problems among other things. When held over a map, it is called map dowsing.

Author's Note:
On the next few pages are a few charts I've devised that can be useful in determining items of importance to your health and spiritual growth. You may use any gemstone that has been placed on a chain or string. Simply dangle the stone over the appropriate chart and ask a specific question. With patience and practice it will sway back and forth or circle above the correct answer. If you feel these charts are too small to work with enlarge the pages on a copy machine at your local print shop.

SECRET MAGICAL ELIXIRS OF LIFE

YES/NO CHART

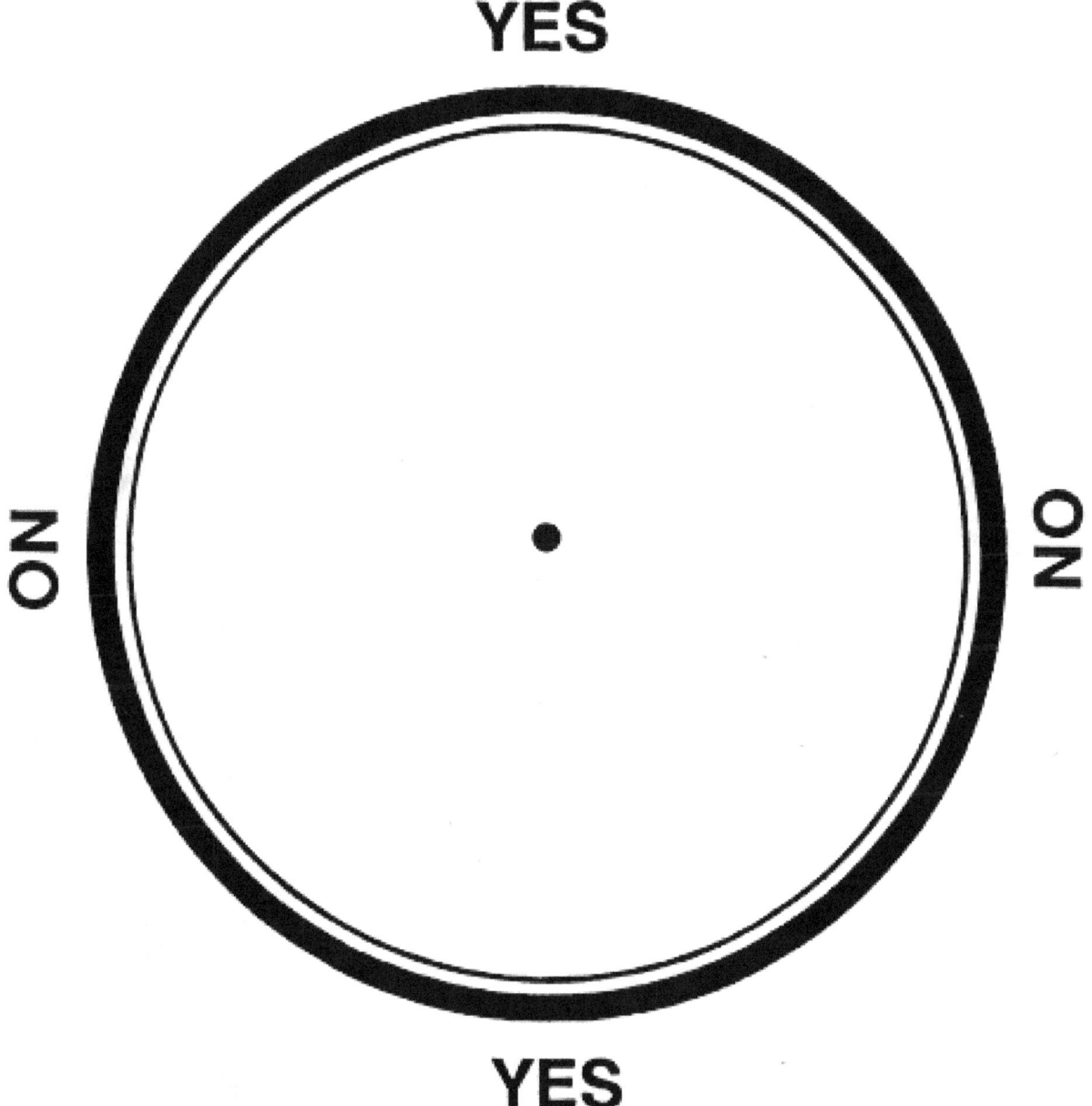

After you have mastered the simple Yes/No chart on this page go on to the next page and use the letters and numbers to spell out answers to your questions.

ALPHABET CHART

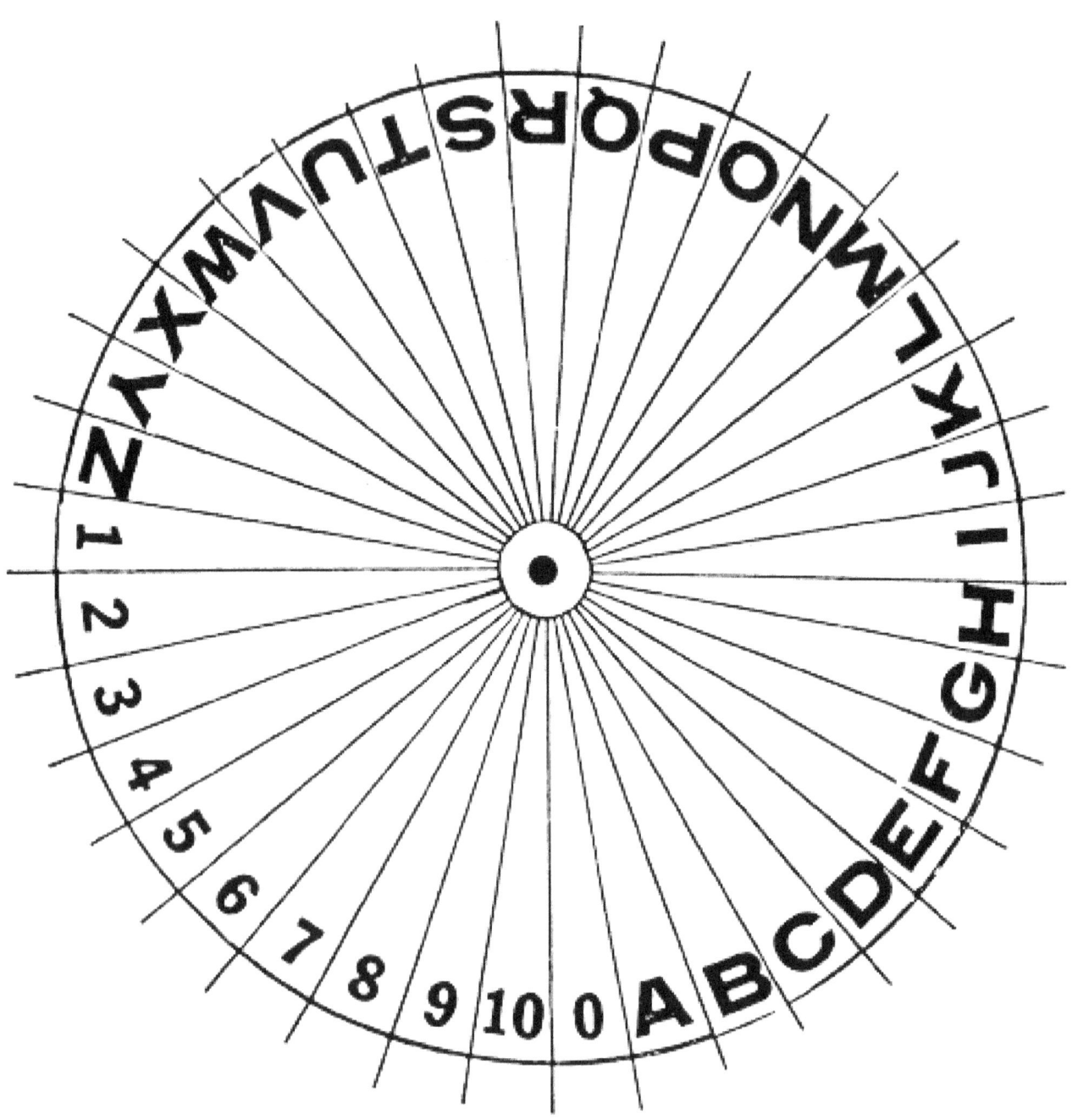

SECRET MAGICAL ELIXIRS OF LIFE

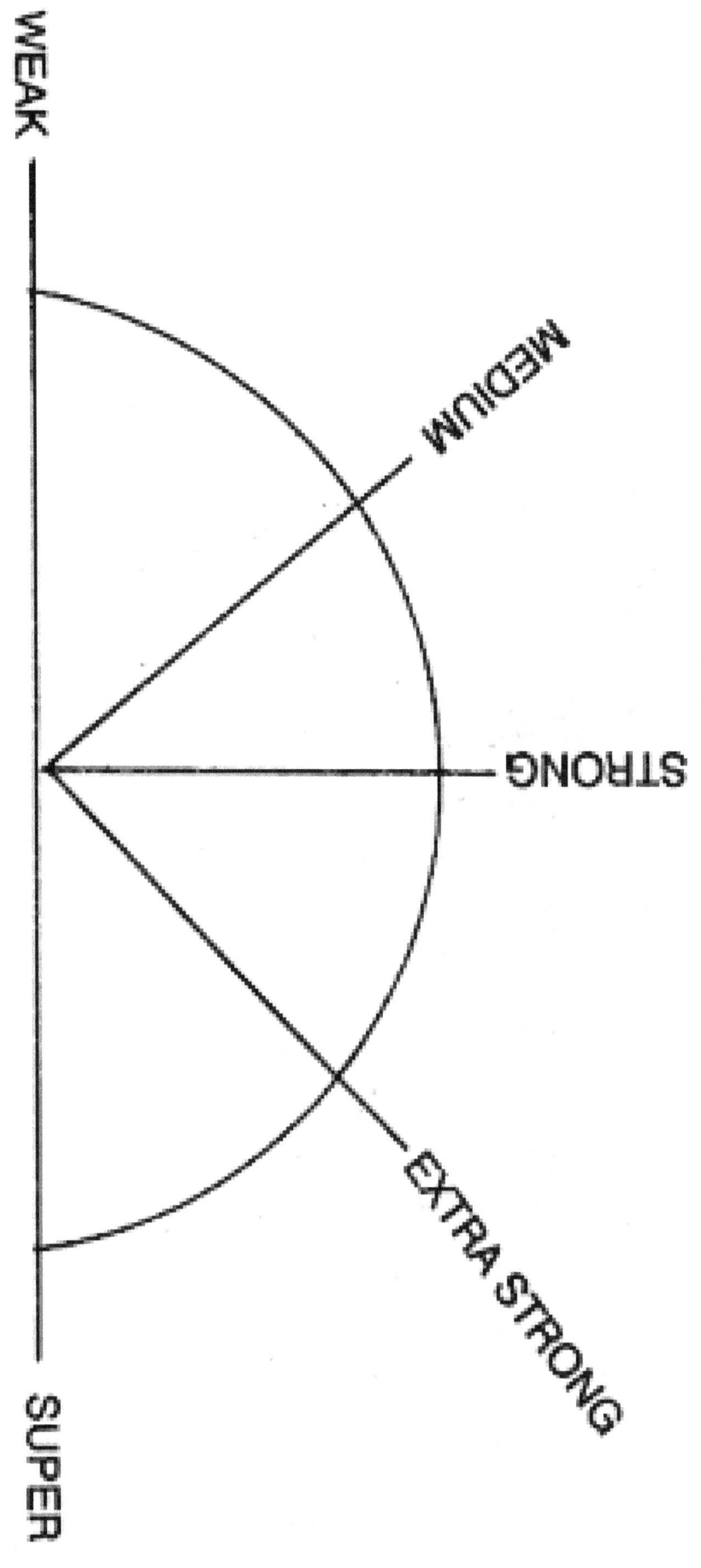

POWERS OF CRYSTALS AND GEMSOTNES CHART

SECRET MAGICAL ELIXIRS OF LIFE

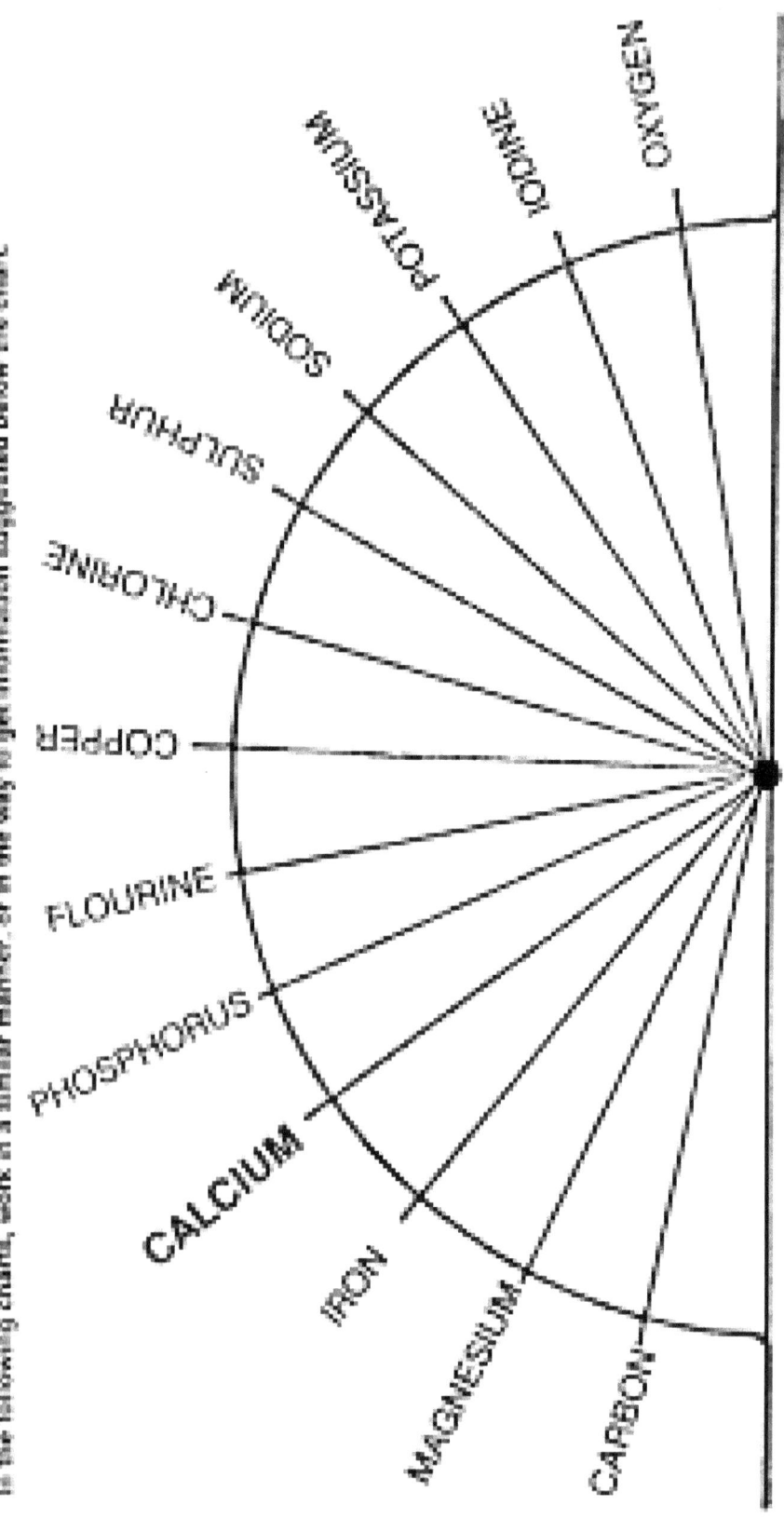

SECRET MAGICAL ELIXIRS OF LIFE

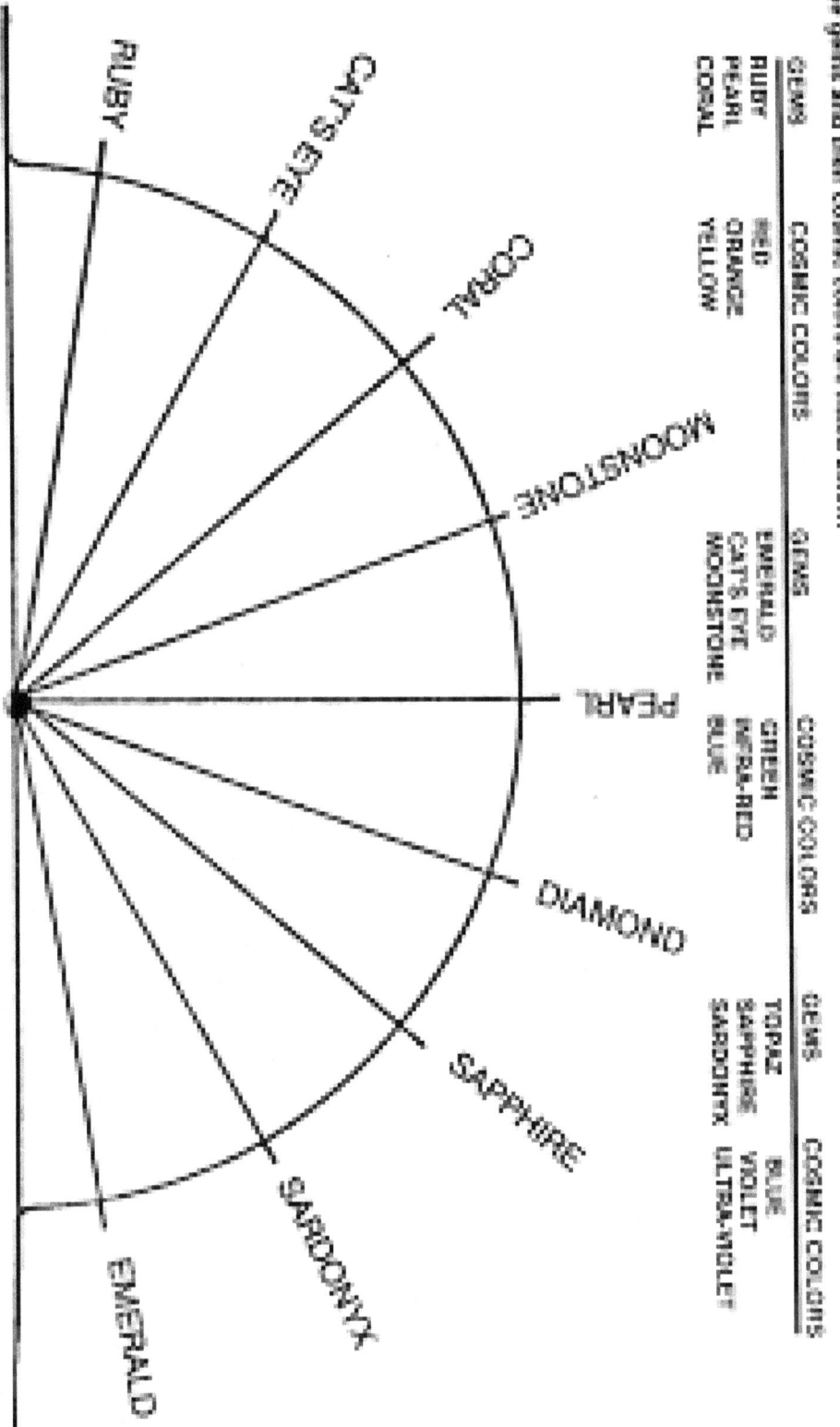

SECRET MAGICAL ELIXIRS OF LIFE

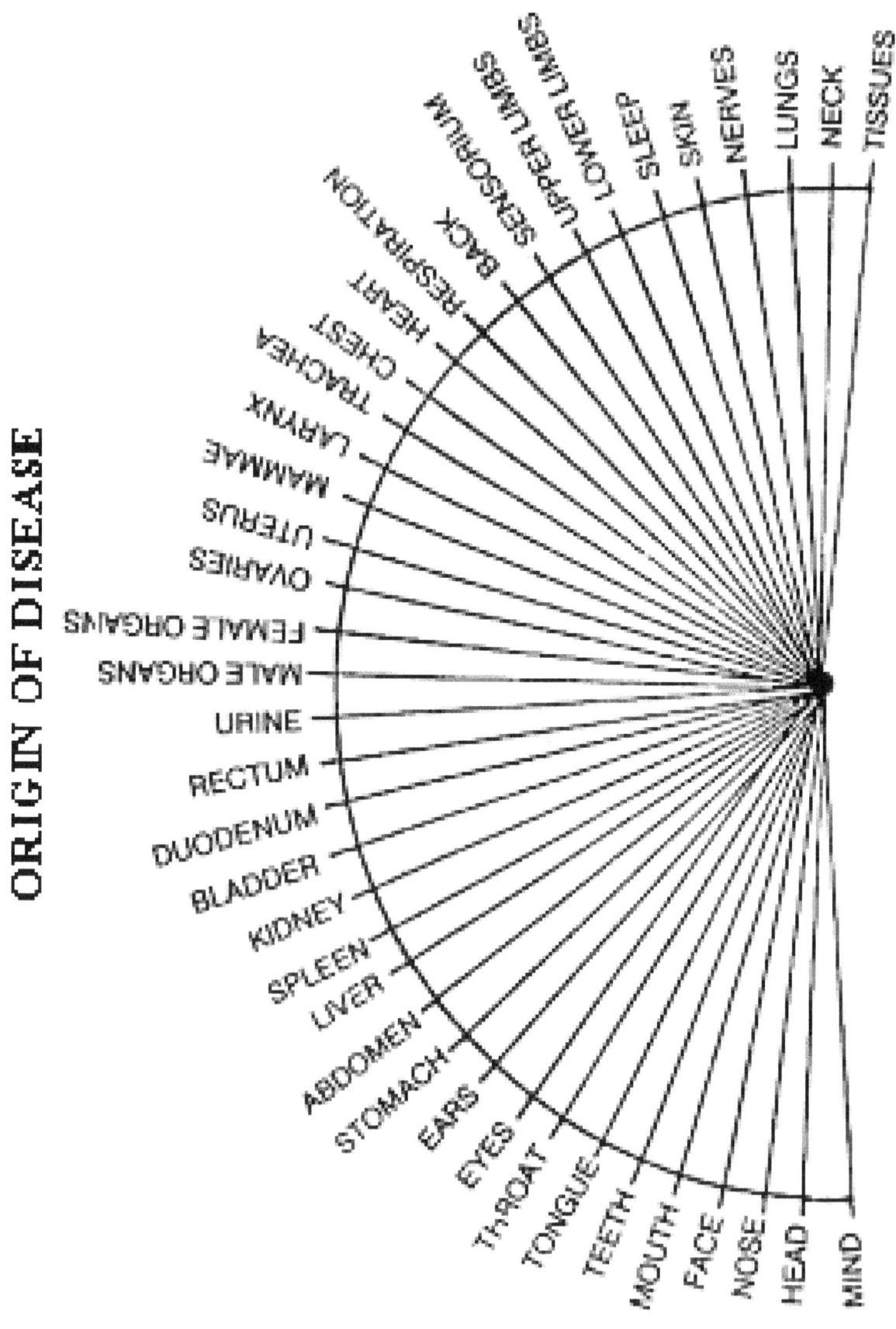

ORIGIN OF DISEASE

SECRET MAGICAL ELIXIRS OF LIFE

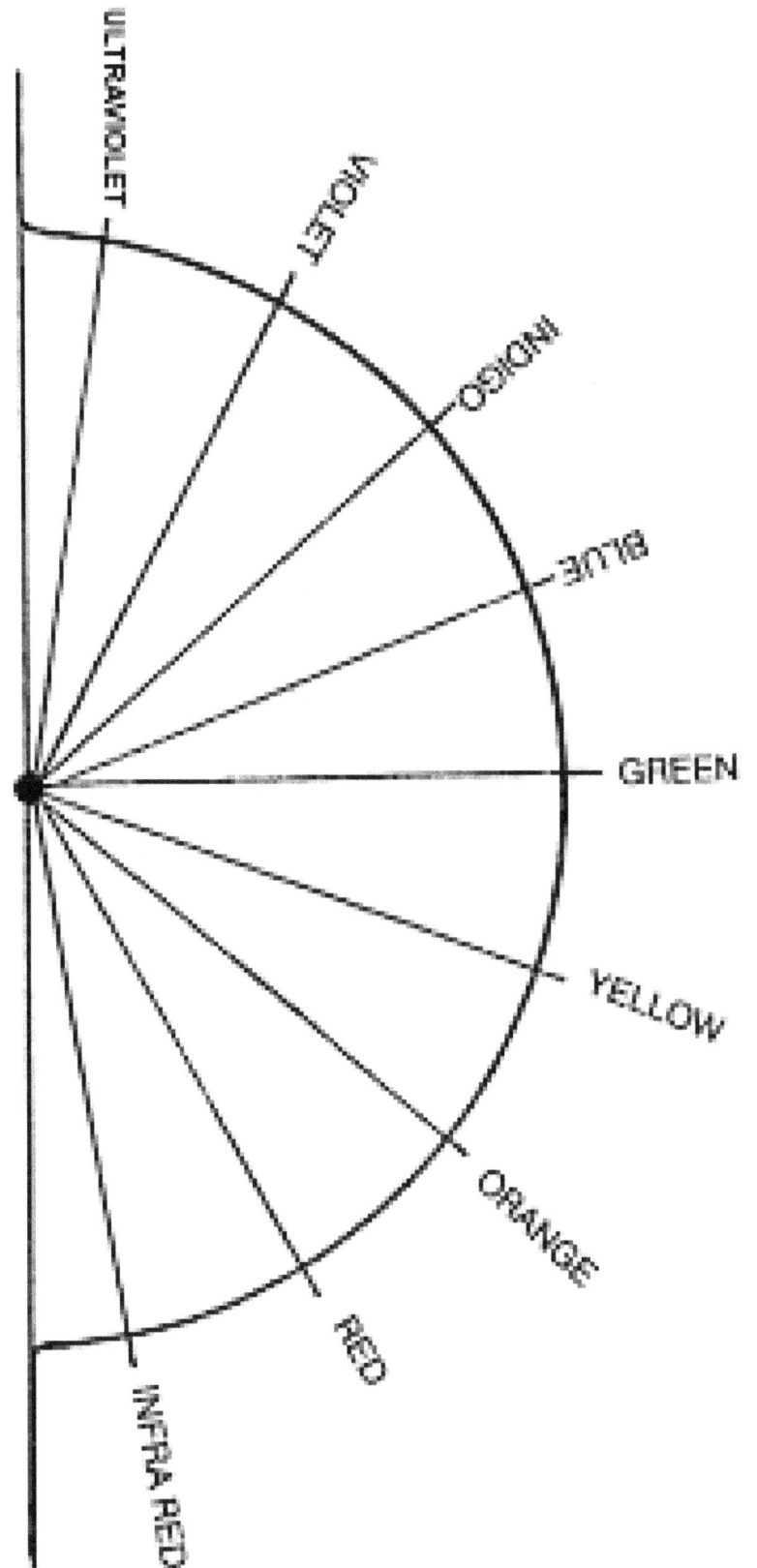

COLOR RADIATION CHART

Color is one of the most important factors in life. Certain colors create, maintain and destroy everything in creation. This will show your predominant color.

The person tested should wear as much of that color as possible and be surrounded with that color at home, for better health.

SECRET MAGICAL ELIXIRS OF LIFE

PERCENTAGE CHART

This chart will check your accuracy, or anything else you may want to know concerning percentages.

Example:
"What is my psychic accuracy?"
"What is my sensitivity?"
"What is my art ability?"

CHAPTER TWELVE

RUNE STONES AS A NEW AGE TOOL

No work on stones would be complete without mention of the casting of Rune Stones and their use as a tool for psychic and spiritual enchancement. Naturally, I have simplified as much as possible the available information, as an entire book could be written about their value and place in the New Age.

The word *rune* has two roots: Germanic - *ru,* and Gothic - *runa,* meaning mystery and secrecy.

The runes are an ancient European form of divination to be able to tell the past, present, and future. On a different level of usage, to work controlled magick.

Here we are more interested in the divination form, since magick would take a complete book in itself.

The Rune Stones are said to predate the Tarot cards, but with certain similarities. Ancient Norse legend tells of the God of Odin as being the original rune master, and it so happens that several Native American tribes have

SECRET MAGICAL ELIXIRS OF LIFE

similar shamanistic rituals. Odin was said, for example, to hang, pierced by spears on the sacred ash tree they named Yggdrasil — the World Tree. On the ninth day without food or water, Odin experienced a surge of insight and received the true knowledge of the runes. You will notice that The Hanged Man in the Tarot cards shows a man hanged upside down, the rope being attached to a wooden gallows. This card represents spiritual enlightenment after suffering.

SECRET MAGICAL ELIXIRS OF LIFE

The Hanged Man

The Magician

The Tower

SECRET MAGICAL ELIXIRS OF LIFE

The meanings are obviously identical. Various religions throughout history have held the belief that suffering brings about spiritual awareness.

We are also able to use the Celtic Cross as a layout for the runes, as well as the Tarot cards. Once you start working with the runes, you will find psychic information flowing easily to you. The stones can also be very definite and detailed in themselves. Due to their ancient origin, they are considered a "trigger" to the Universal Source.

Runes are of Old Germanic origin and can be utilized as an alphabetic letter in communicating with others who can read Old Norse, Gothic, Saxon or Old English. These were used to leave messages between European tribes. You will notice all the runes are straight lines, as this is quicker and easier to write on stones, bones, metal, wood pieces or carved on trees. This alphabet was called Futhork, the name being taken from the first six letters of the runic alphabet. However, this is only a minor part of its usage.

Since ancient times, stones with the runic alphabet were said to be utilized for occult and magickal rites. There is an abundance of poetry in runic form, much the same as many spells are poetic. Our main concern, however, is to be able to find answers to questions that can help better our lives or help us move along the correct path.

The information you receive through Rune Casting is meant to be a guidel. You can either pruchase a set of runes or paint the symbols on small stone pieces after cleansing them, as described in another chapter. Their size does not matter, as long as they are basically uniform. All of the runes being approximately one inch would be fine. There are twenty-five Rune Stones, though some sets have come out with less stones in them. The last Rune stone being a blank.

To do an uncomplicated version of Rune Casting, try the layout with the meanings as given in this book. The meanings are both material and spiritual. Connect your answers depending on your question.

SECRET MAGICAL ELIXIRS OF LIFE

CASTING THE STONES

First place all the Rune Stones face down. Hold your receptive hand, palm down and open, about inch over them. Remember, your receptive hand is the one you do not write with. Close your eyes and ask your question. Example: "Will I make so much money within the next three months?" or "Will my new love relationship work out well for me?" Then pick up six runes, one at a time, and place them face up in the following order.

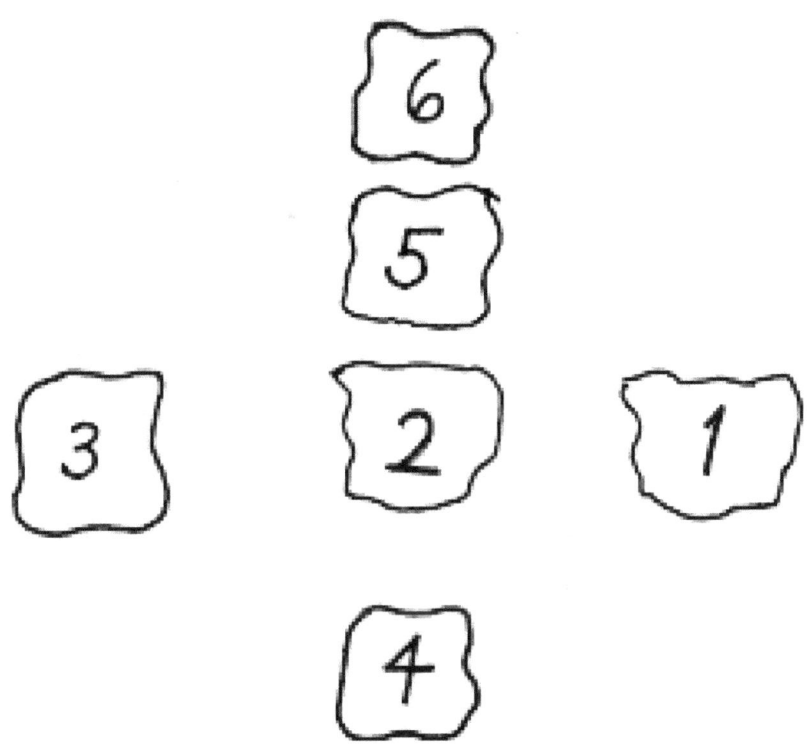

THE RUNE LAYOUT

1st rune — Represents the Past concerning your question.

2nd rune — The situation as it stands Now.

3rd rune — Future factors to be considered.

4th rune — The advice on how to deal with the situation.

5th rune — The obstacle or negativeity concerning the question.

6th rune — The End result.

SECRET MAGICAL ELIXIRS OF LIFE

If you turn the rune over and it is right side up

or leaning toward the right

this means the answer is positive (yes) and you will have success.

If, on the other hand, the rune shows upside down

or leaning left

the answer is negative.

In this case, you need to look at the obstacle. See what it is that you need to change, tone down, or overcome. Then work with the outcome to change it to a more positive result. We receive the information so we can improve our situations.

SECRET MAGICAL ELIXIRS OF LIFE

MEANING OF THE RUNES

 Feoh — Money (fee), Possession, Love, Power.

 Uruz — Health, Knowledge, Power to shape situations.

 Thurisaz — Benefits, Applied power, Force (for destruction or defense).

 Ansuz — Communication, Knowledge, Learning, Inspiration.

SECRET MAGICAL ELIXIRS OF LIFE

Raidho — Success, Career, Travel, Religion, Magick, Spiritual development, Cosmic Law.

Kenaz — Relationships, Sex, Creativity, Friendships, Change.

Gebo — Gift, Balance, Harmony.

Wunjo — Joy, Hope, Harmony.

Hagalaz — Completion, Protection, Unity, Disruptions which are out of your control (flood, tree falling, etc.), Annoyance.

Naudhiz — Protection, Warnings, Constraint - being held back by a situation or others.

Isa — Cooling down emotionally, Standstill.

Jera — A year (12 months), Lessons, Reward, Waiting Period.

SECRET MAGICAL ELIXIRS OF LIFE

Eihwaz		Protection, Endurance, Understanding of the Life and Death Connection.
Pertho		Karma, Change, Luck, Sex (female anatomy).
Elhaz		Protection, Spirituality, Branching out.
Sowilo		Success, Decisions to be made, new beginnings (can be long term).
Tiwas		Victory after self-sacrifice, Explorer, Justice, Spiritual Law and Sex Magick (male anatomy).
Berkano		Home, Family, Protection, Nurturing.
Ehwas		Changes, Marriage, Fertility, Trust.

SECRET MAGICAL ELIXIRS OF LIFE

ᛘ	Mannaz	"I" - represents "Man" (the Divine structure in all men), Knowledge, News.
ᛚ	Laguz	Power, Emotions, Intuition, Psychic input, Growth.
◇	Ingwaz	Direct family (including friends you consider as family), Energy, Fertility.
ᛟ	Othala	Inheritance (material or knowledge), Property on a material level.
ᛞ	Dagaz	Hopes, The Divine Light, Polarity (ie. as expressed by day and night), New beginnings (usually short term).
O	Wyrd	Destiny, Situation not under your control! The unknown.

SECRET MAGICAL ELIXIRS OF LIFE
SAMPLE LAYOUT

ASKING A DEFINITE QUESTION:

Recently a man wanted to know if his decision concerning starting a new business venture was a good one. He really wanted to try it, but being married with a child he had other things to consider, and so he was very hesitant. The question asked was, *"Would it be a positive move to start this business at this time?"*

The following answer came up:

Getting The Answer

1. Ansuz reversed : He lacked the knowledge in the past as well as the initiative to move along this buiness venture.

2. Kenaz : Now there are more positive changes coming into his life.

3. Feoh : In the future he will gain money from the business and will also love what he is doing.

4. Uruz : He now has the needed knowledge, and can control the situation to flow on a positive level.

SECRET MAGICAL ELIXIRS OF LIFE

5. Gebo : The people he will be working with will be difficult to get along with. However, knowing this ahead of time, he can consciously work harder with them, thus, avoiding the problem.

6. Raidho : The outcome if he goes into the new business venture will be success.

Knowing this, he went ahead and was more thoughtful and considerate concerning his employees. They, in turn, started working with him more, since they felt he respected and cared about them. His business is now a success financially, he loves what he is doing, and provides very well for his family.

A general inquiry:

Would you like to know how the upcoming day or month will be? Then ask, "What will today be like for me?" or "What will the following (month, year, etc.) hold for me?"

Use the previous layout. In this example, I asked about a certain date, chose the six rune stones and laid them out in the pattern as illustrated. The following answer is for the day.

SECRET MAGICAL ELIXIRS OF LIFE

1. Uruz reversed : In the recent past few days, this person was not in good health.

2. Ingwaz : However, today he has more energy and will improve due to this.

3. Dagaz : What his hopes are today will be realized in the near future.

4. Laguz : He needs to listen to his intuition to get the most out of today.

5. Ansuz : The obstacle in the way concerns a lack of communication.

6. Wunjo : The day will basically be a happy one.

If this person follows his intuition, and expression of thoughts becomes more detailed, the day will go better. In general, it will be a very positive day.

Working with the runes will also give you a feeling of protection, on the level that you have somewhere to go for insight and information when you have such a need. I find them to be very exact and a great aid in seeking the correct directions in life.

SECRET MAGICAL ELIXIRS OF LIFE

CHAPTER THIRTEEN
MALE AND FEMALE STONES

As mentioned earlier, stones have characteristic vibrations. Some of these vibrations can feel stronger or weaker when being used by persons of different gender. It may be that the stone "blends" with your vibrations rather easily or that the stone itself may have male or female preferences.

Sometimes this can be determined by the warmth of the stone. The ones that are warmer, appear stronger, would tend to be "male", while the female's vibrations would give you a more subtle or toned down feeling.

Whereas the male stone may give off obvious feelings of power, the female stone's power sort of creeps up on you.

Those into metaphysics agree that we will have traits of both sexes in our systems. Most of us have been reincarnated as both males and females. If you are a man and feel you are not sensitive enough, carry a "female" stone. If you are a woman and need to be "stronger," look for a "male" stone to be your companion.

CHAPTER FOURTEEN
STONES AS A SPIRITUAL TOOL

SECRET MAGICAL ELIXIRS OF LIFE

It is very important to cleanse your stones properly. This will enable them to work at full power and energy level.

Upon receiving your stones, you should clean them before use. This is to prevent you from picking up a previous owners negative or positive vibrations.

To clean the stones; put sea salt into a bowl or add it to a glass of water. Place them into the water, then place the bowl or glass on a windowsill or wherever there is sunlight, and leave it there for three days before you use the stones.

Another way is to place the stones into the sea salt and leave them there for a couple of hours. Afterwards, wash them off with running water. They will be ready for use.

When you are storing your stones, keep them in a cloth or pouch. It can be made of any material as long as some air can seep through it.. Make sure you store your stones in areas where no one can touch them or place negative thoughts upon them. By doing this your stones will be safe and clear for your own personal use and influences.

A NEW AGE SCIENCE UNFOLDS

Remember, you can only get out of your stones what you put into them. You must be positive and in turn you will get only beneficial feedback from your crystals or your other gemstones. And don't be afraid to experiment with them as we all have a lot to learn about their use. The New Age Science of "Psychic Gemology" is still in its infancy. For, even though the ancients knew a great deal about their uses and purposes, we are just now beginning to once again unlock the secrets behind the psychic vibrations of crystals, gems and stones.

Conclusion

When God created the world he truly did create everything in it. Just as herbs can be used for healing and for psychic means, so can all the stones that exist right around us.

There is nothing new under the sun, only things that have been neglected or forgotten.

The value of stones is a lot more than many of us have assumed. We cannot think of them as "priceless" in a pure materialistic sense as their vibrations are many fold. Not only have we determined that crystals and gemstones are beautiful to look at, but they are equally beautiful to touch and to hold. This beauty is certainly not just on the surface as their vibrations go to the core of our very being and can help us all to grow to be stronger and more spiritually aware.

Through understanding the nature of stones and how they affect and influence our lives, others, and the world we live in, we obtain a deeper understanding of the Divine Way and its influence upon us.

SECRET MAGICAL ELIXIRS OF LIFE

The four women are carrying symbols which depict each of the four elements of earth, wind, fire and air.

Humanity's spiritual growth could only come about through the understanding and unity of all of earth's elements.

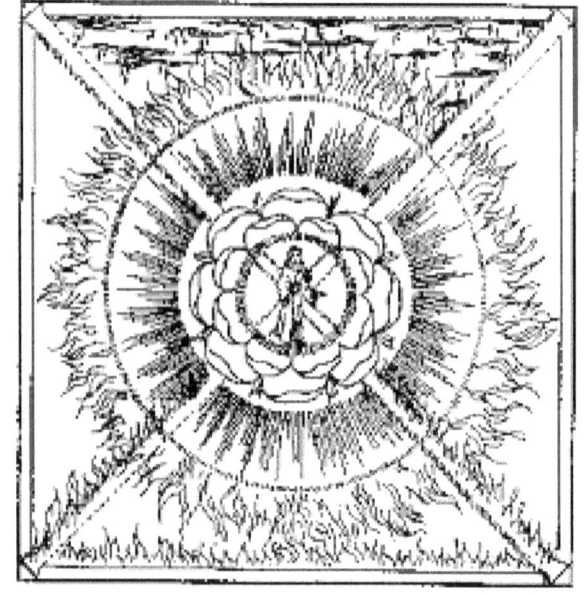

Many of the alchemists of the Middle Ages hid the true meaning of their craft in symbolism lest their secrets fall into the wrong hands.

Glossary

Atlantis:	Ancient submerged civiliztion. Existing, it is believed, in the Atlantic Ocean.
Aura:	Mainly seen by psychics. Energy field surrounding animate and inaminate objects. Has been tested scientifically.
Banish:	To drive away negativity or evil spirits.
Birthstone:	Used in astrology. The theory that stones have a vibrational effect connected to astrological signs you were born under.
Chakra:	Spiritual energy center, connecting to the physical body.
Clairaudience:	The ability to hear sounds other than by our normal means.
Clairvoyance:	Psychic abilities. Mainly considered as a "seeing."
Divination:	Art of getting information by other than our five senses.
Gem elixir:	Placing a mineral stone into water for hours to transfer its vibrations to the water. People drink the water for its benefits.
Kundalini:	Energy, that when raised from the bottom of the spine, in its proper order, gives spiritual enlightenment.
Magick:	Practice of causing changes through the use of power not defined by science.
Mu:	Ancient civilization said to have existed where the Pacific Ocean is now.

SECRET MAGICAL ELIXIRS OF LIFE

Pendulum:
: Tool for divination which entails a heavy object suspended by a string or a chain. Held by a person, it gives answers to questions by its swinging motion.

Power hand:
: The hand you write with. Magickally dominant hand. Used to send out power.

Psychic:
: Referring to the soul, spirit or mind. A person who receives information without the use of the five senses.

Psychometry:
: Ability to receive information from contact with an object directly or indirectly.

Receptive hand:
: Opposite from the hand that you write with. Psychically used to receive information.

Talisman:
: Object worn to protect people from negativity.

Telepathy:
: Sending of thought between people from distances without our normal means.

Visualize:
: To create a mental picture.

ABOUT THE AUTHOR

Rev. Maria D'Andrea was born in Budapest, Hungary. Since early childhood she has demonstrated a high degree of psychic ability. As an Ordained Healing Minister and Pastoral Counselor, Mária has provided excellent psychic guidance and enlightenment to many.

Rev Maria's psychic abilities and talents for over the past twenty-five years include: Crystal Gazing, Rune Casting, Biorhythm, Handwriting Analysis, Numerology, Trance States, Automatic Writing, Occultism, Tarot Card Reading, Kirlian Photography, the teaching of Psychic and Metaphysical techniques and meditation principles and techniques. She is a certified hypnotherapist.

She has been a guest speaker at metaphysical, occult and various organizations throughout the United States. She has also published articles in numerous magazines and professional journals and continues to do so on a regular basis today. Among her credits are numerous appearances on radio and television.

Rev. Maria is the founder of the Sylvan Society—a hermetic order, The Psi Esoteric Guild (TPEG), Spiritrainbow Healing System, as well as The Psi Spiritual And Metaphysical Institute, Founder and Chief Principal Teacher. She is a member of the Spiritual Frontier Fellowship, the Floating Healing Meditation Circle, The Life Study Fellowship, The Psychic Guild, A.R.E. (The Association for Research and Enlightenment), The Ghost Research Society and the Long Island School of Applied Hypnosis. She is a European Shaman and honorary member of the Tucscarora Tribe.

Rev. Maria D'Andrea can be reached at www.mariadandrea.com

SECRET MAGICAL ELIXIRS OF LIFE

Famed Hungarian born psychic tells you which crystals, gems and stones are best suited for your needs. Did you know...not all crystals are the same? Nor do any two stones or gems radiate identical energies. Thus, you may be using the incorrect stones and may not be reaping all the personal benefits of the amazing New Age science of "Psychic Gemology."

Find out which stones are best suited for...HEALING — TELEPATHY — BUILDING A STRONGER AURA - GOOD LUCK — ATTRACTING A SOUL MATE — IMPROVING FINANCES

A professional psychic/lecturer versed in Rune Casting, Tarot, Kirlian Photography and other disciplines. Maria presents dozens of practical tests and experiments you can personally do to test the power of your crystals, gems, and stones, and discover which ones have the highest concentration of power.

SECRET MAGICAL ELIXIRS OF LIFE

NOTES

NOTES

NOTES

SECRET MAGICAL ELIXIRS OF LIFE

OTHER VALUABLE BOOKS BY MARIA D'ANDREA
– ALL LARGE FORMAT WORKBOOKS · EACH INCLUDES A BONUS DVD –

( ) HEAVEN SENT MONEY SPELLS – DIVINELY INSPIRED FOR YOUR WEALTH

Find out why Maria is called "The Money Psychic." Imagine receiving money just by using the powers of your mind. Want a new home? Or pay off an existing mortgage?

Would you like to go on an exotic "dream" vacation with someone who is sexy or your true love? Want to sell the items laying around in your garage or attic for BIG CASH? Interested in picking a large prize lottery ticket, or winning at the tables or slot machines?

Tired of seeing someone else wearing the "Bling?" Diamonds are a girls best friend, but who cares about anyone else when that fabulous stone could be around your finger or neck?

Includes Simple Money Spells DVD— $21.95

Author And Practitioner
Maria D' Andrea

( ) YOUR PERSONAL MEGA POWER SPELLS
Includes Free 60 Minute DVD – "Put A Spell On You 'Cause Your Mine!"

Hundreds of spells that are so powerful their practitioners were once put to death for being witches. Includes spells for protection against unseen forces. Spells for love and romance. Spells for drawing the cornucopia of luck into your life. Spells for creating positive cash flow to enhance your prosperity. Spells for a healthy life. Spells for divining life's purposes with positive magick. Spells for faxing your heart's desires through meditation and visualization. — **$24.00**

EXPLORE THE SPIRITUAL WORLD WITH MARIA - MINI WORKSHOPS AND SEMINARS NOW ON DVD

**Check Off Desired Titles: $10 each
– 3 for $22.00 10 for $79.95
All 16 just $99.95**

1. ( ) **Rearrange Your Life With Positive Energy**
2. ( ) **Adventures Of A UFO Tracker With Tim Beckley And Maria**
3. ( ) **The Amazing Power Of Tesla Energy**
4. ( ) **2012 And Beyond – What Can We Expect?**
5. ( ) **Manifesting A New Reality**
6. ( ) **Exploring The Healer Within You**
7. ( ) **Spiritual And Magickal Runes**
8. ( ) **Soul Mind Dreaming**
9. ( ) **Gemstones How They Rock**
10.( ) **Tap To Manifest**
11.( ) **Angels And The Fall**
12.( ) **A Shamanic Life**
13.( ) **Surrender – Effortless Techniques**
14.( ) **The Power Of Planting Positive Seeds**
15.( ) **Attracting A Relationship**
16.( ) **Gemstones And Your Chakras**

Ordering Information: Each Episode Of **Exploring The Spiritual World Of Maria** is approximately 30 minutes in length and are of broadcast quality. Add $5.00 for S/H.

(Because of their low price these DVDs are shipped in sleeves. Cases not included).

( ) OCCULT GRIMOIRE AND MAGICAL FORMULARY

Cover Art by Carol Ann Rodriguez

Ten books in one! – Over 500 spells! Over 200 oversized pages! With the help of this book you will learn: To manifest your own future destiny. To prevent psychic attack. To use herbal magnets. To apply candle magic to receive individual blessings. To unlock secrets of love potions. To mix the best mystical incense. To draw on the powers of crystals and stones. How prayer really works. The only true application for ritualistic oils. — **$25.00**

( ) SPECIAL OFFER OF THESE 3 BOOKS/DVDS BY MARIA — $59.95 + $8 P/H

**ORDER DIRECTLY FROM:
TIMOTHY G. BECKLEY, BOX 753
NEW BRUNSWICK, NJ 08903**

SECRET MAGICAL ELIXIRS OF LIFE

His Powers Are Unsurpassed In The West
T. Lobsang Rampa "Miracle Man"

TWO TITLES NEVER RELEASED IN NORTH AMERICA!
NEW! BEYOND THE TENTH
RAMPA HAS DECLARED . . .

OVER TEN MILLION BOOKS SOLD WORLDWIDE!

"Man is one tenth conscious, the other nine tenths deal with the subconscious and all that which comes under the heading."

"THIS BOOK IS ABOUT YOU! NOT JUST ABOUT ONE TENTH OF YOU, BUT ALSO THAT WHICH GOES BEYOND THE TENTH"

For many years the famous author and occult master has been asked thousands of questions from both students and admirers from all over the world. They all want to know how they can better their own lives and how they can bring about a global spiritual revolution which would include all of humankind, not just one political group or religious sect.

Every half million years (give or take) the earth sees fit to shuck off its stock, as it goes about preparing the surface of the planet for the next bunch, whom it hopes might be more successful in living in harmony with nature and the cosmic plan.

If you are traumatized by the insanities of our times T. Lobsang Rampa may provide you with some ways to calm your nerves and confront the devils that seek to stifle our every movement and prevent us from becoming the individual we were meant to be.

BEYOND THE TENTH is a rally cry for what is transpiring all around us. Come and join the "party" and free yourself from the manacles of self imposed human slavery.

BEYOND THE TENTH is the favorite work of many Rampa fans. Order now for just **$18.00**

NEW! CANDLELIGHT
ANSWERS ARE FINALLY GIVEN — THE TRUTH ABOUT RAMPA'S TRANSMIGRATION

Cynicism has always been a part of the author's existence. Those that disbelieve who T. Lobsang Rampa says he is will never be convinced otherwise.

Those that believe need to be offered nothing additional in the way of evidence.

In this wonderfully fulfilling work, the great mystic reveals the truth about transmigration and how he went for being an ordinary plumber (or was he?) to one of the most remarkable men in the world of mysticism:

Says Tuesday Lobsang Rampa about this puzzling phenomenon:

"Transmigration is stated to be the movement of one soul from one body into another body. There are many, many recorded instances in the world's history in which the soul of a person has departed from a body but before death occurred to that body another body was taken over. It is as simple as that."

Get ready to be propelled in an out of this world experience. Here are little known facts about reincarnation, including who you were and who you might be in the future. Understanding is the key to expanding your consciousness and opening your heart and mind to the universe. Rampa will guide you.

JUST FOLLOW THE FLICKER OF THE CANDLELIGHT!
For your personal copy of Candlelight just send **$18.00**

SPECIAL OFFER
BOTH NEW TITLES JUST $32.00 + $5.00 S/H

MORE RAMPA TITLES
Large Format Editions
Check Desired Items -- Just $20 Each

( ) **THE THIRD EYE** - This is the book that started it all back in the 1950s, revealing Rampa's psychic abilities.
( ) **THE HERMIT** - A dark cavern holds great wisdom from the ancients.
( ) **THE RAMPA STORY** - Secrets of the Lama's life revealed to the outside world.
( ) **MY VISIT TO AGHARTA** - Journey to the capitol of the underground at the center of the earth.
( ) **DR FROM LHASA** - Wonders and secrets from the Top Of The World!
( ) **TIBETAN SAGE** - Practical uses of Shamanism and powers of the Monks.
( ) **CAVE OF THE ANCIENTS** - Revealing secrets of ancient space ships, lost civilizations, and anti gravity.
( ) **CHAPTERS OF LIFE** - How to make the most out of "hard times."
( ) **LIVING WITH THE LAMA** - 25 years of a cat who telepathically "talked" with TLP.
( ) **SAFFRON ROBE** - Astral travel adds to life's journey of the soul. Rampa leads the way.
( ) **TIBETAN SAGE** - Return to the Hall of Records and the Cave of the Ancients.
( ) **TWILIGHT** - Hidden chambers beneath the earth explored.
( ) **FLIGHT OF THE PUSSYWILLOW** - Mrs Rampa gives her joyful view of worldy events.

SPECIAL ALL 15 RAMPA BOOKS THIS PAGE $249.00 + $12 S/H

RARE RAMPA MEDITATION AND PRAYER AUDIO CD
This is a one of a kind recording - the only know "record" with Rampa's voice on it. Runs approx 40 minutes. Join in his celebration of life. $12.00

Available Now From:
TIMOTHY G. BECKLEY · BOX 753
NEW BRUNSWICK, NJ 08903
Pay Pal Orders use mrufo8@hotmail.com
Credit Cards 732 602-3407

SECRET MAGICAL ELIXIRS OF LIFE

Maria D'Andrea

Now On Dvd! A Guide To Practical Spirituality And How To Make Things Happen

MARIA D' ANDREA'S SPIRITUAL LIFE COUNSELING MINI WORKSHOPS
Effortless And Immediate Metaphysical/Psychic Techniques That Work

Let The Most Gifted Of Psychics And Spiritual Counselors Transform Your Life Into A Fountain Of Abundance

Maria D' Andrea, MsD., D.D., DRH is an internationally known professional psychic from Budapest, Hungary. Since early childhood she has demonstrated high spiritual awareness and psychic ability. Maria is a Shaman, a Metaphysician, and a Psychic Consultant

SERIES NO. ONE
3 DVD SET - $21.95

Disc # 1 – THE POWER OF PLANTING SPIRITUAL SEEDS

Maria teaches how to utilize your thoughts in a creative way so that each action becomes a most powerful tool for change. This is an excellent DVD to create positive transformations in your life.

Disc # 2 — YOU CAN LEARN TO LIVE A SHAMANIC LIFE

One of the many exercises in this DVD is trusting your first instinct. Experience a journey from beginner to master and tap into hidden knowledge so your ordinary life turns into a shamanic one.

Disc # 3 – DEVELOPING THE HEALER WITHIN YOU

Discover the hidden healer within. Here are the basic principles that allows anyone to become self empowered in the healing arts. Use for your own well being and the health of your loved ones.

SERIES NO. TWO
3 DVD SET - $21.95

Disc # 1 – ATTRACTING RELATIONSHIPS

Maria teaches how to draw more positive relationships in today's world. Learn the importance of applying ancient methods to enhance your opportunities. She also explains the power of colors, gemstones and astrological periods that are best for women and men.

Disc # 2 – SURRENDER YOURSELF TO A POSITIVE LIFE

Discover how to allow spirit to assist you in having a more exciting life. Maria teaches the importance of releasing yourself from the past, while empowering you so that you can create your future as the present moment.

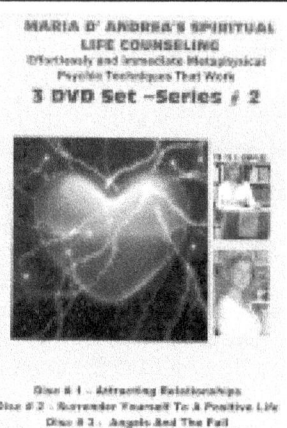

Disc # 3 – ANGELS AND THE FALL

As a Hungarian spiritual and psychic metaphysician, Maria explains the various angels and how they can assist us. She reveals the meaning and importance of shielding to assist in working with these all powerful beings. Maria shows you how to work with Archangel Ariel and Zavael with specific techniques. This DVD helps to calm the storm in your life and to create a more positive being.

VERY SPECIAL OFFER
ALL 6 DVDs JUST $39.00 + $5 S/H
ORDER FROM:
Timothy Beckley • Box 753
New Brunswick, NJ 08903
credit card order hot line:
732-602-3407

www.ingramcontent.com/pod-product-compliance
Lightning Source LLC
Chambersburg PA
CBHW081921170426
43200CB00014B/2799